What the Foucault?

What the Foucault?

Marshall Sahlins

PRICKLY PARADIGM PRESS
CHICAGO

First edition published as *Waiting for Foucault* in 1993 by Prickly Pear Press; second edition, 1996; third edition, 1999. Fourth edition published as *Waiting for Foucault, Still* in 2002 by Prickly Paradigm Press.

Prickly Paradigm Press, LLC
5629 South University Avenue
Chicago, IL 60637

www.prickly-paradigm.com

ISBN: 978-0-9966355-4-7
LCCN: 2017957326

Printed in the United States of America on acid-free paper.

Being After-Dinner Entertainment by Marshall Sahlins for the Fourth Decennial Conference of the Association of Social Anthropologists of the Commonwealth, Oxford, 29 July 1993. Now in an expanded, fifth edition.

Lord Jenkins, Professor Strathern, Dear Colleagues... and other Colleagues:

I have been charged by Professor Strathern with providing "after-dinner entertainment" in thirty minutes or less, presumably so that you will not be found sleeping when Professor Stocking delivers his Huxley Lecture. I don't know what I have done to deserve this high academic honor, still less how to live up to it, except that like many of you I keep a note-book of underground observations, ranging from one-liners to many-pagers, from which I thought to offer you a selection of curmudgeonly remarks on what's up nowadays in Anthropology and probably shouldn't be. At the outset, however, I have to confess that in looking over my notebook it struck me that Lord Keynes didn't tell the whole story about the long run. At least as far as Anthropology goes, two things are certain in the long run: one is that we'll all be dead; but another is that we'll all be wrong. Clearly, a good scholarly career is where the first comes before the second. Another thing that struck me, and helped inspire my lecture title, was that this notebook was a lot like Michel Foucault's sense of power—poly-amorphous perverse. So it is in that post-structuralist spirit that I offer the following *pasticherie* for your dessert.

The Invention of Tradition

Since Britain is the homeland of "the invention of tradition" I hardly need to explain the phrase. You also know that anthropologists have rushed to adapt the idea to the current nostalgia for culture amongst the erstwhile colonial peoples. The third- and fourth-world over, people are proclaiming the values of their traditional customs (as they conceive them). Unfortunately a scholarly air of inauthenticity hangs over this modern culture movement. The academic label "invention" already suggests contrivance, and the anthropological literature too often conveys the sense of a more or less counterfeit past, drummed up for political effects, which probably owes more to imperialist forces than to indigenous sources. As a possible antidote, I call your attention to a remarkable invention of tradition, whose respectability no Western scholar will be tempted to deny.

For it happens that in the 15th and 16th centuries a bunch of indigenous intellectuals and artists in Europe got together and began inventing their traditions and themselves by attempting to revive the learning of an ancient culture which they claimed to be the achievement of their ancestors but which they did not fully understand, as for many centuries this culture had been lost and its languages (Latin and Greek) had been corrupted or forgotten. For centuries also these Europeans had been converted to Christianity, but this did not prevent them from now calling for the restoration of their pagan heritage. They would once again practice the classical virtues, even invoke the pagan gods. All the same, under the circumstances—the great distance of the acculturated intellectuals from a past that was effectively irrecoverable—under the circumstances, nostalgia was not what it used to be. The texts and monuments they constructed were often ersatz facsimiles of classical models. They created a self-conscious tradition of fixed and essentialized canons. They wrote history in the style of Livy, verses in a mannered Latin, tragedy according to Seneca and comedy according to Terence; they decorated Christian churches with the facades of classical temples and generally followed the precepts of Roman architecture as set down by Vitruvius—without realizing these precepts were Greek. All this came to be called the Renaissance in European history, because it gave birth to "modern civilization."

What else can one say about it, except that some people have all the historical luck? When Europeans invent their traditions—with the Turks at the gates—it is a genuine cultural rebirth, the beginnings of a progressive future. When other peoples do it, it is a sign of cultural decadence, a factitious recuperation, which can only bring forth the simulacra of a dead past.

On the other hand, the historical lesson could be that all is not lost.

(*Journal of Modern History*, Spring 1993)

On Materialism

Materialism must be a form of idealism, since it's wrong—too.

Heraclitus vs. Herodotus

One of the current arguments against the coherence of cultures and the possibility of doing any kind of systematic ethnography is that, like a certain famous philosophical river, cultures are always changing.

Such is the flux that one can never step in the same culture twice. Yet unless identity and consistency were symbolically imposed on social practices, as also on rivers, and not only by anthropologists but by the people, there could be no intelligibility or even sanity, let alone a society. So to paraphrase John Barth, reality is a nice place to visit (philosophically), but no one ever lived there.

Post-Structuralism

This is a modern American folk-tale to the same effect: Three umpires of major league baseball were debating how to call balls and strikes, "I calls 'em the way they is," the first said. "Me," said the second, "I calls 'em the way I sees 'em." "Naw," declared the third, who had been around the longest, "they ain't nothin' till I calls 'em." Technically, according to the *Cours de gymnastique générale*, this is known as the "arbitrary character of the umpire's sign". Whence comes the post-structuralist dictum, "Don't be Saussure." (Eric Hamp)

Item: *Chicago Tribune*, May 23, 1993: Jim Lefebvre became the first manager ejected in the history of Joe Robbie Stadium with Friday night's incident. Plate umpire Ed Rapuano did the deed after Lefebvre protested a called third strike on Sammy Sosa. "The ball was down", said Lefebvre... "When he kicked me out, he said 'I don't care where the pitch was.' He doesn't care where the pitch was? Big-league umpire!"

Japanese Culture is Always Changing

A Japanese friend said of the famous imperial shrine at Ise that it is unchanged since the 7th century, the same as it was when it was first built. Of course, it doesn't look that old to Westerners. But according to the current tradition, the buildings at Ise have been rebuilt (in alternating sites) every twenty years in exactly the same way—using the same ancient instruments and the same materials—with each step of the process marked by the appropriate ancient rituals. Of course, the instruments couldn't be exactly the same, could they? They haven't lasted for thirteen centuries. And what does it mean to say the materials are the same, since new wood is used each time? And are two ritual performances ever "the same"?

(In fact, the rebuilding cycle was once interrupted for more than 150 years, and the buildings and tools have seen some changes. But that is not the dominant Japanese tradition or perception. The tradition is that they are unchanged and the perception is they are the same.)

One Western art critic explains that the rebuilt buildings are not "replicas" but "Ise re-created."

Perhaps something close to the Shinto conception, since nature is indeed involved, would be our concept of the continuity of a forest: the Amazon forest could be in existence for centuries or millennia, even though every one of the original trees is gone, has been replaced many times. In any case, it is obvious that identity is a relative construction, based on a selective valuation of similarities and differences. At Ise, it is irrelevant that the materials have been renewed—thus to Western eyes "not the same"—so long as they are of the same type and put together under the ancient ritual and technical regime. By such criteria, what we call Tinturn Abbey could not pass under that name, the age and "authenticity" of the stones not withstanding. It would not be Tinturn Abbey, because it is a ruin.

In his life of Theseus, Plutarch tells the following story about the ship on which the hero returned to Athens after slaying the Minotaur: The thirty-oared galley in which Theseus sailed with the youths and returned safely was preserved by the Athenians down to the time of Demetrius of Phalerum (317- 307 BC). At intervals they removed the old timbers and replaced them with sound ones, so that the ship became a classic illustration for the philosophers of the disputed question of growth and change, some of them arguing that it remained the same, and others that it had become a different vessel.

And what should we make of the popular observation that "culture is always changing"?

Etics and Emics

All etics or languages of objective scientific description (so-called) are based on a grid of meaningful or emic distinctions. Take the international phonetic alphabet, by means of which the significant sounds of any language can be "objectively" recorded and reproduced. The phonetic alphabet is made up of all known phonemic distinctions: of all differences in sound-segments known to signify differences in meaning in the natural languages of the world. So in principle the objective description of any language consists of its comparison with the meaningful order of all other languages.

The same for ethnography. No good ethnography is self-contained. Implicitly or explicitly ethnography is an act of comparison. By virtue of comparison ethnographic description becomes objective. Not in the naive positivist sense of an unmediated perception—just the opposite: it becomes a universal understanding to the extent it brings to bear on the perception of any society the conceptions of all the others. Some Cultural Studies types—Cult Studs, in Tom Frank's description—seem to think that Anthropology is nothing but ethnography. Better the other way around: ethnography is Anthropology, or it is nothing.

The Poetics of Culture, I

Anthropologists wanted. No experience actually necessary. Make more than most poets.

The Poetics of Culture, II

In speaking of culture as a superorganic order, in which individuals counted for next to nothing, A.L. Kroeber liked to use the metaphor of a coral reef: a vast edifice built by tiny microorganisms each of which, acting simply according to its own nature, secretes an imperceptible addition to this structure whose scale and organization by far transcends it. Just so in culture:

Lives of great men all remind us
We can make our lives sublime,
And in passing leave behind us...
A small deposit of lime.

"The Pseudo-Politics of Interpretation" (Gerald Graff)

In a recent issue of the vanguard journal *Cultural Anthropology* a certain cultural relativism was dismissed as (I quote) "politically unacceptable." Similarly, a summary comment to a recent book of essays on Polynesian history warns that Geertz's *Negara* and Sahlins's Polynesian works, by their attempts to understand history in such terms as culture or structure afflict the study of others with "dangerous" notions: that is, essentializing notions that falsely endow a people with eternal cultural qualities, or overvalue hegemonic ideologies by neglecting "the politically fractured and contested character of culture." Dangerous? Hopefully the day is not far off when this kind of terrorism will seem patently lunatic. In the meantime, however, the best intellectual argument is the moral-political high ground. To know what other peoples are, it suffices to take the proper attitudes toward sexism, racism and colonialism. As if their truth was our right-mindedness. Or as if the cultural values of other times and places, the events they organized and the people responsible for them, were fashioned in order to answer to whatever has been troubling us lately. But (I paraphrase Herder) these people did not suffer and die just to manure our little academic fields.

And surely it is a cruel post-modernist fate that requires the ethnographer to celebrate the counter- hegemonic diversity of other people's discourses— the famous polyphony or heteroglossia—while at the same time he or she is forced to confess that shis own scholarly voice is the stereotypic expression of a totalized system of power. It seems that imperialism is the last of the old-time cultural systems. Ours is the only culture that has escaped deconstruction by the changing of the avant garde, as it retains its essentialized and monolithic character as a system of domination. So anthropologists can do nothing but reproduce it. Advanced criticism thus becomes the last refuge of the idea that the individual is the tool of shis culture. Which also proves that those who are ignorant of their own functionalism are destined to repeat it—the second time as farce.

Utilitarianism

A people who conceive life to be the pursuit of happiness must be chronically unhappy.

In Adam (Smith)'s Fall, Sinned We All

The punishment was the crime. By disobeying God to satisfy his own desires, by putting this love of self before the love of Him alone that could suffice, man was condemned to become the slave of insatiable bodily desires: a limited and ignorant creature abandoned in an intractable and merely material world to labor, to suffer, and then to die. Made up of "thorns and thistles," resistant to our efforts, the world, said Augustine, "does not make good what it promises: it is a liar and deceiveth." The deception consists in the impossibility of assuaging our libidinous desires for earthly goods, for domination and for carnal pleasures. So man is fated "to pursue one thing after another, and nothing remains permanently with him...his needs are so multiplied that he cannot find the one thing needful, a simple and unchanging nature."

But God was merciful. He gave us Economics. By Adam Smith's time, human misery had been transformed into the positive science of how to make do with our eternal insufficiencies: how to derive the most possible satisfaction from means that are always less than our wants. It was the same Judeo- Christian Anthropology, only bourgeoisified, and on the whole a somewhat more encouraging prospectus on the same investment opportunities afforded by human suffering. In a famous essay setting out the field, Lionel Robbins explicitly recognized that the genesis of Economics was the economics of Genesis. "We have been turned out of Paradise," he wrote, "we have neither eternal life nor unlimited means of satisfaction"—instead, a life of scarcity, wherein to choose one good thing is to deprive oneself of another. The real reason Economics is dismal is that it is the science of the post-lapsarian condition. And the Economic Man inhabiting page one of (any) *General Principles of Economics* textbook is Adam.

The Poetics of Culture, III

Power, power everywhere,
And how the signs do shrink.
Power, power everywhere,
And nothing else to think.

The current Foucauldian-Gramscian-Nietzschean obsession with power is the latest incarnation of Anthropology's incurable functionalism. Like its structural-functional and utilitarian predecessors, hegemonizing is homogenizing: the dissolution of specific cultural forms into generic instrumental effects. It used to be that what you had to know about prescriptive joking relations—their *"raison d'être" même*—was their contribution to maintaining social order, even as totemic ceremonies or garden magicians were organizing food production. Now, however, "power," is the intellectual black hole into which all kinds of cultural contents get sucked, if before it was "social solidarity" or "material advantage." Again and again, we make this lousy bargain with the ethnographic realities, giving up what we know about them in order to understand them. As Sartre said of a certain vulgar Marxism, we are impelled to take the real content of a thought or an act as a mere appearance, and having dissolved this particular in a universal (here economic interest), we take satisfaction in believing we have reduced appearance to truth. Max Weber, criticizing certain utilitarian explanations of religious phenomena, observed that just because an institution may be relevant to the economy does not mean it is economically determined. But following Gramsci and Foucault, the current neo-functionalism of power seems even more complete: as if everything that could be relevant to power were power.

Quite wondrous, then, is the variety of things anthropologists can now explain by power and resistance, hegemony and counter-hegemony. I say "explain" because the argument consists entirely of categorizing the cultural form at issue in terms of domination, as if that accounts for it. Here are some examples from the past few years of *American Ethnologist* and Cultured *(Cultural) Anthropology*:

1. Nicknames in Naples: "a discourse practice used to construct a particular representation of the social world, [nicknaming] may become a mechanism for reinforcing the hegemony of nationally dominant groups over local groups that threaten the reproduction of social power."

2. Bedouin lyric poetry: this is counter-hegemonic.

3. Women's fashions in La Paz: counter-hegemonic.

4. The social categorization of freed Dominican slaves as "peasants": hegemonic.

5. The fiesta system of the Andes in the colonial period: hegemonic.

6. The constructed "spirituality" of middle-class Bengali women, as expressed in diet and dress: hegemonic nationalism and patriarchy.

7. Certain Vietnamese pronouns: hegemonic.

8. Funeral wailing of Warao Indians, Venezuela: counter-hegemonic.

9. Do-it-yourself house building of Brazilian workers: an apparent counter-hegemony that introduces a worse hegemony.

10. The scatological horseplay of unemployed Mexican-American working class males: "an oppositional break in the alienating hegemony of the dominant culture and society."

11. Common sense: "common sense thought and feeling need not tranquilize a restive population but can incite violent, if contained, rebellion."

12.The concept of culture as a seamless whole and of society as a bounded entity: hegemonic ideas that have "effectively masked human misery and quenched dissenting voices" [quenched? Give us then your tired and your thirsty].

"A hyper-inflation of significance" would be another way of describing the new functionalism, translating the apparently trivial into the fatefully political by a rhetoric that typically reads like a dictionary of trendy names and concepts, many of them French, a veritable La Ruse of postmodernism. Of course the effect, rather than amplifying the significance of Neapolitan nicknames or Vietnamese pronouns, is to trivialize such terms as "domination," "resistance," "colonization," even "violence" and "power." Deprived of real-political reference, these words become pure values, full of sound and fury and signifying nothing...but the speaker.

Courses for Our Times

A colleague at the University of Chicago, expert in material culture, offered a course on "Chicago Blues," under the general heading "The Intensive Study of a Culture," a portmanteau rubric for undergraduate courses devoted to the presentation of recent ethnographic research. I was prompted to put the following notice on the departmental bulletin board, thinking if Chicago Blues was a culture, Michigan football could also be one—that I have done intensive research in.

INTENSIVE STUDY OF A CULTURE:
MICHIGAN FOOTBALL

Anthropology 21215
Saturday, 1:30 - 4:30 pm
Extra Credit for New Year's Day
Instructor: Marshall Sahlins

Anthropology 21215. Intensive Study of a Culture: Michigan Football. *PQ: Undergraduates only; limit of 10.* Because of the impossibility of pure presence, the course materials will consist of video transmissions—considered however in their textuality. There can be no pretence of a totalized or master narrative of Michigan football, only a consideration of certain aporias of the Power-I formation—which is to say, of postmodern subjectivity. Selected topics include: trash-talking or contested discourses; tight ends, spread formations and other subject positions; post Gerry-Fordism or de-center subject; post-deconstruction and other victory celebrations; and the helmet essentialism. *M. Sahlins. 1:30-4:30 Sat, extra credit for New Year's Day.*

But that was not the funny thing. The funny thing was how many students, including graduate students, took it seriously, believed there really was such a course, and e-mailed asking to sign up for it. One person wondered if I could employ him as a teaching assistant. After the quarter was over, another four people asked how the course went. Scary!

Relevance

I don't know about Britain, but in America many graduate students in Anthropology are totally uninterested in other times and places. They say we should study our own current problems, all other ethnography being impossible anyhow, as it is just our "construction of the other."

So if they get their way, and this becomes the principle of anthropological research, fifty years hence no one will pay the slightest attention to the work they're doing now. Maybe they're onto something.

Polyphony is not Cacophony
(for Maurice Bloch)

Malama Meleisea tells of taking down two completely different and conflicting stories about the history of certain Samoan chiefs from the lips of one and the same matai (chiefly title holder). When confronted with the discrepancies, the matai reminded Meleisea that he held titles in two different villages, and if Malama would recall he told the first story in one village and the second in the other. So obviously he was speaking as one chief the first time and as a rival chief the second. And what was so inconsistent about that? One is reminded of the Cartesian dictum about clear and distinct ideas—I mean Hocartesian, of course, not to be mistaken for the essentialist doctrines of Descartes—the Cartesian dictum that in Fiji two contradictory statements are not necessarily inconsistent. "They appear to us contradictory," Hocart said, "because we do not know, without much experience, the point of view from which each is made."

But we are not likely to hear an end soon to post-structuralist litanies about the contested and unstable character of cultural logics: about perceptions and meanings that are different for men and women, chiefs and commoners, rich and poor, old and young, this village and that, yesterday and today—as if a difference were necessarily a disorder. All the same, not everything in the contest is contested (which also proves we come here to paraphrase Durkheim, not to bury him). As polyphonic or heteroglossic as the monograph may be one does not find a Japanese voice in a Sioux Indian ethnography. In order for the categories to be contested at all, there must be a common system of intelligibility, extending to the grounds, means, modes and issues of disagreement. The differences at issue, moreover, entail some relationship. All the more so if they are subversive and thus express the positional values and interests of speakers in a certain social-political order. As Cassierer says in another context, "an awareness of a difference is an awareness of a connection."

The alternative is to suppose that what people say is arbitrary and aleatory from the point of view of their social existence—in which case, it is true, there could be nothing like anthropological knowledge, or for that matter a social existence. But if in regard to some given event or phenomenon, the women of a community say one thing and the men another, does not the difference in what they are saying express social differences in the construction of gender: their discrepant positions in, and experience of, a certain social universe? If so, there is a non-contradictory way—dare one say, a totalizing way?—of describing the discrepancy. There is some system in and of the differences. Bakhtin did not for a minute suppose that the presence of dissenting voices was unsystematic. What he said was that in combination with the authoritative discourse, such heteroglossia produced a more complex system.

Culture as a Metaphysical Pseudo-Entity

Some grave conclusions have been drawn from the fact that anthropologists cannot agree on what "culture" is, the most serious being that the culture concept is an artifact of a certain historical period, logically incoherent and "loaded willy nilly with ideological baggage and unconscious associations peculiar to particular sets of historical circumstances" (Christopher Herbert). Something as bad as that, one would think, ought to be dumped as soon as possible.

And should we not do the same with money? "Money" is a totally elusive concept—even harder to hold onto, I think, than "culture." Economists and economic historians cannot agree on a definition of money. The differences among them on the nature of money make the Kroeber-Kluckhohn collection of culture-definitions seem like an enviable consensus. And matters get even worse when we interview the natives.

In practice, "money" is a specious notion if ever there was one, a contested category without determinate bounds or content. Rich and poor, old and young, men and women, clergy and laity, poets and scientists, psychoanalysts and sane people: all have so many irreconcilable opinions about whether money is good or bad, about what it can or cannot buy, whether or not it can make you happy, how it is related to love, politics, beauty, justice, friendship, the human soul, and whatnot.

A lot of people, mostly people without a lot of money, say that money can't buy everything. Especially it can't buy happiness: people with 25 million, for example, are not perceptibly happier than people with 24; and besides, rich people are generally unhappy. Still the rich have many consolations, as Plato observed—the chief among them presumably being their money. And despite the fortitude it takes for the rich to endure their disadvantages (Rex Stout), most modern philosophers agree that money is better than poverty—"if only for financial reasons," as Woody Allen speculates. This conclusion has also been persuasively argued on controlled empirical grounds by Sophie Tucker: "I've been rich and I've been poor; rich is better."

Some deep epistemological uncertainties likewise attend the argument that money can't buy knowledge, a proposition that the educational costs and outputs of American private universities make excruciatingly problematic. A modern Jewish proverb, however, has it that although money won't make you a physicist, it does help you like reality.

The Christian pecuniary theology, incidentally, is another heteroglossic nightmare. New Testament views about the relation between evil and the love of money are well known, but there is more than a suggestion of heresy in the popular paraphrase that "the want of money is the root of all evil." Regarding Abe Lincoln's observation that "God must love the poor or He wouldn't have made so many of them," H.L. Mencken replied, "He must love the rich or he wouldn't divide so much mazuma among so few of them."

All this suggests that money is a prototypical fuzzy category. Ever subject to conflicting discourses, the concept of money is constantly being undermined by a politics of interpretation in which hegemonic norms are challenged by dissenting voices. It follows that the meaning of money in relation to other things, the Saussurean value of the category, is always shifting. Consider the categorical entanglements of "money" and "sex." When we say that someone is well-fixed or well-endowed, what exactly are we talking about? The ambiguities are succinctly summed up by Zsa Zsa Gabor: "What I call loaded, I'm not; what other people call loaded, I am."

Obviously the concept of money, on which Economic Science has been running, is highly artificial, historically particular and profoundly ideological. I say "ideological" because the promulgation of this fiction, in the same way as the promulgation of the essentialist doctrine of culture, has evident colonizing effects. Clearly the spread of the money concept is useful to the imperialist ambitions of Western capitalism. Yet just as the totalized notion of "culture" constructed by anthropologists, this "money" is a metaphysical phantom, fundamentally and incurably equivocal. Money, like culture, is a pseudo-entity. And a fool is easily separated from both.

Consciousness of Culture

The word "culture" has become common fare. For the present generation it does much of the work that was formerly assigned to "psychology" or again "ethos." We used to talk about "the psychology of Washington (D.C.)" or "the ethos of the university;" now it is "the culture of Washington" and "the culture of the university." It is also "the culture of the cigar factory," "the culture of drug addiction," "the culture of adolescence," "the culture of the Anthropology meetings," etc. For a long while I was worried about this apparent debasement of the anthropological object. One day I realized that Economics is still going as a discipline despite that everyone talks about "economics," and "economies," Sociology likewise survives all the uses of "social." And recently I saw the following poster in a hotel elevator: "50 hotels, 22 countries, one philosophy." You think we got troubles with "culture?" What about Philosophy? Everybody's got a philosophy. It didn't kill Philosophy.

Orientalism
(dedicated to Professor Gellner)

In Anthropology there are some things that are better left un-Said.

How to Solve the World's Problems

There is a sure, one word solution to most of the world's current problems: Atheism.

The Chinese Restaurant Syndrome

Why are well-meaning Westerners so concerned that the opening of a Colonel Sanders in Beijing means the end of Chinese culture? A fatal Americanization. Yet we have had Chinese restaurants in America for over a century, and it hasn't made us Chinese. On the contrary, we obliged the Chinese to invent chop suey. What could be more American than that? French fries?

Anthropology as Cultural Critique

If Anthropology is really cultural critique, we might as well bring back Hobbes or Rousseau, who were at least aware that they were inventing an antithetical Other for salutary political purposes.

Waiting for Foucault

"A man of a thousand masks," one of his biographers said of Michel Foucault, so how seriously can we take the guise he assumed to say that power arises in struggle, in war, and such a war as is of every man against every man. "Who fights whom?" he asked. "We all fight each other." Critics and exegetes hardly notice Foucault's connection to Hobbes except to mention the apparently radical disclaimer that his own notion of power is "the exact opposite of Hobbes' project in *Leviathan*." We have to give up our fascination with sovereignty, "cut off the king's head," free our attention from the repressive institutions of state. Power comes from below. It is invested in the structures and cleavages of everyday life, omnipresent in quotidian regimes of knowledge and truth. If in the Hobbesian contract subjects constitute the power, the Commonwealth that keeps them all in awe, in the Foucauldian schema power constitutes the subjects. All the same, the structuralism that Foucault abandoned for a sense of the poly-amorphous perverse, this structuralism taught that opposites are things alike in all significant respects but one. So when Foucault speaks of a war of each against all, and in the next breath even hints of a Christian divided self—"And there is always within each of us something that fights something else"—we are tempted to believe that he and Hobbes had more in common than the fact that, with the exception of Hobbes, both were bald.

Objectivity as a Secondary Quality

According to the basic Enlightenment epistemology, knowledge is objectively grounded by interest, i.e., pleasure and pain, which thus gives us the truth conditions for the properties of things. Why hasn't anyone mentioned that this proof-of-the-pudding empiricism makes all objective knowledge the knowledge of "secondary qualities" in the Lockean sense? The objectivity of objects is relative to a body whose construction determines what is pleasurable and painful; and beyond that, insofar as this body is socially constructed, it is relative to the cultural order. The same would follow from the obvious principle that it is impossible to exhaust the empirical description of anything, inasmuch as it can be known by its relations to an indefinite number of other things; hence the objectivity of the object is always selective.

This is what makes the referential use of signs tricky, since such uses may well be perceptually true, hence seemingly natural, though never necessary. For the French the distinction of *fleuve* and *rivière* is that between an inland waterway that flows to the sea and a substantial tributary thereof, thus incommensurable with SAE "river" and "stream" which refer simply to waterways of different scales (Jonathan Culler). Yet the French usage is no less an objective-empirical difference for all that it is not the only possible one. Locke said that men would not have it thought that they speak idly of the world; but this does not prevent them from constituting the world variously, "according to the Manners, Fashions and Customs of the Country." The French are hung up on where the sea is. Paris, an inland city, has right and left banks. Maybe it's because England is there.

More on Materialism

Hence the contradiction that Anthropology has been living with for some time, viz., that symbolicity encompasses the material determination of the symbolic.

Some Laws of Civilization

First law of civilization: All airports are under construction.

Second law of civilization: I'm in the wrong line.

Third law of civilization: Snacks sealed in plastic bags cannot be opened, even using your teeth.

Fourth law of civilization: The human gene whose discovery is announced in *The New York Times*—there's one every day, a gene *du jour*—is for some bad trait, like schizophrenia, kleptomania, or pneumonia. We have no good genes.

Fifth law of civilization: Failing corporate executives and politicians always resign to spend more time with their families.

Cultural Relativism

The concept of "cultural relativism," properly understood, has not outlived its usefulness. What is useless is
the vulgar sense of relativism to the effect that the
values of any society are as good as, if not better than,
the values of any other, including our own. Properly
understood, cultural relativism is an anthropological
technique for understanding cultural differences, not a
charitable way of granting moral absolution. It consists
of the provisional suspension of our own moral judg-
ments or valuations of other people's practices in order
to place them as positional values in the cultural and
historical contexts that gave rise to them. The issue is
what these practices mean, how they came about, and
what their effects are for the people concerned, not
what they are or are worth in our terms.

In this same relativist regard, the local people's onto-
logical scheme, their sense of what there is, must likewise be considered in itself and for itself, and not
distorted by analytic concepts that substitute our
certainties of "reality" for theirs. Take the category of
"myth," for example. In standard average English, to
label statement as "myth" means it's not true. Hence
in speaking of other people's "myths," we characteristically assert that what they know as sacred truth, and
upon which they predicate their existence, is fictional
and unbelievable—for us. Having thus debunked the
constitutional basis of their society—as in the ethno-
logical oxymoron, "mythical charter"—we are given
liberty to write it off as essentially unreal for them too:
an epiphenomenal mystification of their actual socio-
political practice. What is then typically left to the

scientific project is a more or less feckless search for the "kernel of historical truth" in a narrative riven with irrelevant fantasy—in this way ignoring that the concepts thus devalued are the true history at issue. For taken in that veridical capacity by the people concerned, the so-called "myth" is truly organizing their historical action. Myth is not an ideological after-thought so much as it is a historical precedent.

Relations of Society = Symbolicity

It is intriguing how many of the dispositions usually attributed to human nature are intrinsic conditions of symbolic discourse—and have in that regard some claims to universality without the necessity of biology. This seems especially evident in the sociology of the linguistic "shifters": "I" and "you," "here" and "there," "now" and "then," etc. The person using the pronoun "I" thereby constitutes space, time and objects (reference) from his or her point of view—egotism, or even the will to power. One's interlocutor does the same, an alternative assertion of world-making authority—competition. The same alternation recognized as the reversibility of "I" and "you,"—reciprocity or altruism. The mutuality of personhood implied by this interchange of subject positions—sociability. Symbolic discourse contains within itself the elementary principles of human social interaction.

Postmodern Terrorism

One of the more poignant aspects of the current post-modernist mood is the way it seems to lobotomize some of our best graduate students, to stifle their creativity for fear of making some interesting structural connection, some relationship between cultural practices, or a comparative generalization. The only safe essentialism left to them is that there is no order to culture.

Capitalism I

Marx said, "the country that is more developed indus-
trially only shows, to the less developed, the image of
its own future." In large part, however, this prediction
would still fall under Durkheim's dictum that "a
science of the future has no subject matter."

Capitalism II

In the same vein, in a century increasingly marked by the indigenization of modernity, Max Weber's comparative project on the possibilities for capitalist development afforded by different religious ideologies seems increasingly bizarre. Not that it is bizarre to talk of the cosmological organization of practical action, which is surely one of Weber's greatest ideas. What seems increasingly weird is the way Weberians became fixated on the question of why one society or another failed to evolve this *summum bonum* of human history, capitalism—as Westerners have known and loved it. In 1988, when I was in China, this topic was evoking a lot of Confucian. I heard one visiting American sinologist observe that during the Qing dynasty China had come "oh so close" to a capitalist take-off. Yet it all seems like asking why the Highland peoples of New Guinea failed to develop the spectacular potlatch of the Kwakiutl. This is a question the Kwakiutl social scientist could well ask, since with their elaborate pig exchange ceremonies between clans the New Guineans had come so close. Nearer the point—or perhaps it is exactly the point—is the Christian missionaries' question of how it could be that Fijians in their natural state failed to recognize the true god. One might as well ask why European Christians did not develop the ritual cannibalism of Fijians. After all, they came so close.

Capitalism III:
Laissez Faire—Qui les a laissé?

It should not be forgotten that the theory of the most coercive and totalized institution known to humanity, the theory of the state, is the corollary and remedy of a condition of unrestrained self- interest—as in Hobbes, or for that matter St. Augustine. The theory reminds us that an enormous system of social control is required to maintain the *laissez-faire*, the "free" play of self-interest, of a capitalist nation-state. To think otherwise would be like supposing that the feudal knights once charging around the countryside had fashioned their own armor and mounted their horses all by themselves.

Conspiring in Western Violence and Domination

We are warned—by Akhil Gupta and James Ferguson, for example—that by celebrating the historical creativity of the indigenous peoples in the face of globalization, we ignore the tyranny of the world system and conspire thus in Western violence and domination. On the other hand, it is clear that when we speak of the systematic hegemony of imperialism, we ignore the peoples' struggles for cultural autonomy and conspire thus in Western violence and domination.

The dilemma is compounded by the fact that both hegemony and resistance are demanded by the current politics of anthropological interpretation. Ever since Gramsci, posing the notion of hegemony has entailed the equal and opposite discovery of the resistance of the oppressed. So the anthropologist who relates the so-called grand narrative of Western domination is also likely to subvert it by invoking "weapons of the weak," "hidden transcripts" or some such local discourse of cultural defiance. In any case, this is a no-lose strategy since the two characterizations, domination and resistance, are contradictory and in some combination will cover any and every historical eventuality.

Economic Development

Developing countries, with American help, never develop.

Economic Development II

Economic development is properly defined as the material enrichment of the people's way of life. Their culture is the object of development, not the impediment.

Culture of Resistance; Resistance of Culture

There is much talk nowadays about "cultures of resistance" though clearly what is going on among many victims of Western imperialism is better described as the resistance of culture. Moreover, such resistance has been going on for a long time, before and apart from Western imperialism. Involving the integration of the foreign in categories and relations of the familiar—a shift in the cultural contexts of external forms and forces that also changes their values—cultural subversion is in the nature of intercultural relations. As a mode of historical differentiation inherent in meaningful action, this sort of cultural resistance is more inclusive than any intentional opposition, as it neither requires a self-conscious politics of cultural distinction nor has it been historically confined to the reactions of the colonially oppressed. (Recall the theoretical genealogy that leads from the ordering of Boasian diffusions of "culture traits" by Benedictine "patterns of culture," through Bateson's determinations of "schismogenesis" in culture contacts, to the similar dialectics of complementary differentiation in Lévi-Strauss's *Mythologiques*). But pre-colonial culture change apart, even the subjects of modern dependency relations act in the world as social-historical beings. To paraphrase Freud on Marx, they do not all of a sudden become conscious of who they are when they get their first paycheck. Rather, the forces of capitalist hegemony, mediated by the habitus of specific forms of life, are then played out in the schemata of alien cultural universals.

The Indigenization of Modernity

The globalization mavens—both in the academy and in the economy—who are now calling upon us to transcend the observation that local societies indigenize the global order are the same ones who first told us to ignore the possibility.

Whatever Happened to "Late Capitalism"?

It became neo-liberalism.

Man, the Hunter—and the Former Journal

All across the northern tier of the planet, hunters and gatherers still exist—many of them by hunting and gathering. In Northern America particularly, they have harnessed industrial technologies—snowmobiles, CB radios, motorized fishing vessels, modern weapons and camping gear, even airplanes—to their traditional "paleolithic" purposes and relationships. As late as 1966, however, anthropologists at the famous "Man, the Hunter" conference at Chicago thought they were talking about an obsolete way of life. Some years later, Richard Lee, one of the original conveners, remarked at another such conference: "Hunting is real. Hunting exists and hunting and gathering economies exist, and this is to me a new fact in the modern world, because twelve years ago at the 'Man, the Hunter' conference we were writing an obituary of hunters." Indeed the title of the 1966 conference now seems as out-of-date as its contents. Today one could not possibly have a conference called "Man, the Hunter." It would have to be something like, "The Journal of the Royal Anthropological Institute, the Hunter."

Return of the Superorganic

Post-structuralism, post-modernism and other "afterological studies" (Jacqueline Mraz) sometimes come down to a sense of cultural coercion, a narrative of hegemony so totalizing, as to put one in mind of the superorganic theory of culture promoted by Leslie White in the 1940s and 50s. (As a student, I knew it well.) In White's view, culture was an independent, self-moving order of which human action was merely the expression. The individual, White wrote, is in this respect like a pilotless aircraft controlled from the ground by radio waves. Yet substitute "culture" for "discourse" in the following passage from the up-to-date Foucault and we are right back to the obsolete White: "In short, it is a matter of depriving the subject (or its substitute) of its role of originator and of analyzing the subject as a variable and complex function of discourse" ("Post-structuralist Studies," M.H. Abrams wrote recently, "whatever their disagreements, coincide in abstracting literary texts from the human world and relocating them in a nonhuman state—specifically in the play of language—as such, or else in forces that operate within a discourse already-in-being"). Indeed a good many anthropologists have been content to trade in "culture" for Foucauldian "discourse" in recent years—all the while disdaining the "reified" "essentialized" and "totalized" character of the old culture concept. It seems a fair bargain. As the "process through which social reality comes into being," or again a "system" that "determines what can be thought and said," as one anthropological Foucauldian recently put it, such "discourse" seems at least as terrorist as the old-time culturology. Selectively dictating what can be perceived, imagined and expressed, "discourse" is the new superorganic—made even more compelling as the effect of a "power" that is everywhere, in all quotidian institutions and relations.

One wonders if White and Kroeber could have gotten away with their cockamamie theories longer if they had developed a sense of people being the moral victims of the "superorganic."

Dead White Whales: From Leviathanology to Subjectology, and Vice Versa

The opposition between Man and the City, between private and polis interest, is already present in classical writings: in several dialogues of Plato as well as many passages of Thucydides. In Thucydides the opposition is notably grounded in a self-regarding human nature driven by desires of glory and gain. The simple-minded sociological dualism of this counterposition of individual and society, the sense of a transparent and unmediated relationship between them, was likewise destined to have a brilliant historical career. Individuals in particular and society in general confronted each other over an empty social space, as though there were no institutions, values and relationships of diverse character that at once connected and differentiated them. This ancient simplicity continues in the latest, most advanced notions of societal constraint, such as Althusserian interpellation or Foucauldian power. True these speak of mediating structures, but only to assign them the singular function of transmitting the larger order of society into the bodies of individuals.

Along the way to modernity, as it passed through early Christianity, the classical individual-society dualism had absorbed a heavy moral charge, making the conflict well nigh irreconcilable. Pericles might reasonably argue that individuals could best achieve their own happiness by submitting themselves to the public good. In the Christian version, however, the earthly city was no longer Athens but the residence of inherently sinful man; hence the absolute positive value of society as a providential instrument of repression. For

St. Augustine, the social control of unruly bodies—of the child by the father, as of the citizen by the state—was a necessary condition of human survival in this contemptible world of Adamic self-pleasers. Otherwise, men would devour each other like beasts. For a mythico-philosophical translation of the same, see Hobbes. For a modern sociological version, Durkheim. Man is double, Durkheim said, double and divided: composed of a moral cum intellectual self, received from society, struggling to hold in check an egocentric and sensual self that is essentially pre-human. But Durkheim is not really modern. This idea of man as half angel, half beast is archaic.

Modern is the more imperialist philosophy that attempts to encompass one side of the ancient dualism in the other: subsuming the individual in the society or else assuming the society in the individual; such that in the end only one of the pair has any independent existence. Either society is no more than the sum of relations between enterprising individuals, as Jeremy Bentham and Margaret Thatcher would have it; or individuals are nothing more than personifications of the greater social and cultural order, as in certain progressive theories of the construction of subjectivity by power that amount to the death of the subject. The development of capitalism and its discontents gave the old anthropological dualism still another twist, specifically political and in some ways dialectical. Right and Left pushed each other into complementary and extreme arguments of individual and cultural determinism. On the Right, rational choice theory and other such brands of Radical Individualism: all content to resolve social totalities into the projects of self-fashioning individuals. On the Left, concepts of the cultural superorganic and other species of Leviathanology: draconian notions of autonomous cultural behemoths with the powers of fashioning individual subjects to their own purposes.

Radical Individualism is the everyday self-consciousness of bourgeois society; Leviathanology is its recurrent nightmare. Supposing that the values actually originating in the society are, as the means and ends of utilitarian action, attributes of the subject, Radical Individualism suppresses the social and cultural as such—ontologically, as Louis Dumont says. Conversely, Leviathanology dispenses with the subject as such, since he or she merely personifies the categories of the social-cultural totality, and shis actions carry out its independent laws of motion. The famous liberal ideology of the Invisible Hand already harbored these antithetical anthropologies in its obeisances to the great objective social mechanism that mysteriously transformed the good that people did for themselves into the well being of the nation. *Laissez-faire* thus included its negation. And if Adam Smith & Co. could argue for the freedom of individuals to indulge their natural propensity to truck and barter, on the ground that the social good would automatically follow, the critique of capitalism countered by rendering visible this self-subsisting Great Pumpkin with the power of encompassing and conjugating the behavior of individuals in ways beyond their power and control. Thus Marx, in the Preface to *Capital*:

> Here individuals are dealt with only insofar as they are personifications of economic categories, embodiments of particular class-relations and class interests. My standpoint, from which the evolution of

> the economic formation of society is viewed as a process of natural history, can less than any other make the individual responsible for relations whose creature he remains, however much he may subjectively rise above them.

In the early 20th century, the "superorganic" Anthropology of Kroeber and White indeed envisioned a great cultural critter, with people as it were trapped in its belly as it proceeded on its own course. "Behold now the behemoth…he is a king over all the children of pride." Here was a primary source of that ominous sense of culture as an authoritarian prescription of conduct: especially self-defeating conduct, as in the so-called culture of poverty or the "traditional culture" that keeps "underdeveloped peoples" from becoming happy just like us. But even the advanced leviathanological discourses of Althusser and Foucault retained characteristics of the terrific ancestor, employing a pervasive sense of repression without contradiction in their constructions of subjectivity without agency.

Foucault especially. The most awesome transubstantiation of that old holy ghost, the Invisible Hand, into an all-controlling culture-at-large, would have to be Foucault's pancratic vision of power. Here is power as irresistible as it is ubiquitous, power emanating from everywhere and invading everyone, saturating the everyday things, relations and institutions of human existence, and transmitted thence into people's bodies, perceptions, knowledges and dispositions. The theoretical effect of this vision, many critics agree, is not merely "an overestimation of the efficacy of disciplinary power," but "an impoverished understanding of the individual which cannot account for experiences that fall outside the realm of the 'docile' body" (L. McNay). Foucault rightly denies he is a structuralist, since all that is left of structuralism in his problematic is its avoidance of human agency. His position is indeed "post-structuralist," inasmuch as it theoretically dissolves the structures—families, schools, hospitals, philanthropies, technologies, etc.—into their instrumental effects of discipline and control. It is the classic acid bath of functionalist wisdom, reducing the actual substance of the institution to its conjectured purposes and consequences. Also classic is the effective resolution of the problem to the simple society-individual dualism. Indeed, it all ends with the return of the repressed individual—Subjectology.

For with this dissolution of cultural orders into subjugation effects, the only thing left standing, the only thing substantively remaining to the analysis, is the subject into whom these totalities have been interpolated—or the subject thus interpellated. The effect is indeed ironic because the original project of Leviathanology, insofar as it was opposed to Radical Individualism, was to reduce the individual subject to nullity. But in the upshot, all the structures having been erased as such in favor of their instrumental effects, the subject is the only thing left with any attributes of agency or efficacy. Hence the return of the very metaphysics of the subject that the analysis had meant to deny. Suddenly the pages of the up-to-date journals are filled with all kinds of subjects, subjectivities and selves, thus with an Anthropology in the form of allegory, telling tales of cultural forms and forces in terms of abstract collective persons. Taking the place of the structures is a whole new cast of characters, featuring bourgeois subjects, national subjects, postmodern subjects, late capitalist subjects, colonial subjects, post-colonial subjects, postcolonial African subjects, not to forget "the easily recognized wounded subject of the modern liberal state." Then too there are the Cartesian selves and the Melanesian selves, the neo-liberal selves and the subaltern selves, plus a whole population of subjectivities: globalized, hybridized, creolized, modernized, commoditized and otherwized. It is a brave new world that has such people in it. Just as ancient mythologies could represent cosmic forces in anthropomorphic guises, so in the pages of scholarly journals these abstract personifications of cultural macrocosms now strut and fret their hour upon the stage doing…what, exactly?

Well, if not exactly nothing, not too much it seems. Occasionally there are inflated claims: as those made of a certain "late socialist subject," who according to an article in *Public Culture* was the "source" and "inner logic" of the collapse of the Soviet Union. Or curious promises, as those of certain practitioners of "progressive social theory," concerned "with the status and formulation of the subject, the implications of a theory of the subject for a theory of democracy." But it is difficult to see how such concern for the subject can compensate for the historical formations and dynamics that have thus been anthropomorphized. All we get is postcolonial subjects who resist (but in what determinate way?); colonial subjects who are disciplined or repressed (again, in what way?); bourgeois subjects who are alienated or wounded (like you and me?) or else who commodify (what?) or consume (what?); national subjects who identify (with what?), or other such tautological people. If a cultural or historical analysis were really wanted, one would have to return to the structural conditions that had been lost in the translation to subjective terms.

Nor will the liturgical invocation of "multiple subject positions" do much good. Either the multiplicity is resolved into pure individualism, since in principle there are as many subject positions as there are individuals; or it replicates Leviathanology in general by generating a school of whales, a collection of essentialized, collective persons instead of the one giant one. Either way, Leviathanology ends up in the tautology with which Radical Individualism began: with an abstract and ideal subject possessing the whole kingdom of social ends in the form of his or her own private ends. In the theoretical event, all the evils that were supposed to belong to culture, essentialization, totalization and their ilk, also got transferred to this poor shnook.

Subjectology Continued

The secret is that Culture and Personality is back. "Subjectivity" is nothing new. Recall Ruth Benedict's *Patterns of Culture*, which "patterns" turn out to be collective-subjective dispositions. (Just as essentialized as the more recent subjectivities, they are also as much in need of Lacanian psychoanalysis.) *The Chrysanthemum and the Sword*, for that matter, is an unsung classic of Subjectology. And how 'bout good ole "national character"?

As in the perennial opposition of individual and society, of which this is a version, subjectivity is always shadowed by its collective, superorganic negation. Leviathanology and Subjectology are in endless oscillation. To paraphrase Marx, culturology has never gone beyond the antithesis between itself and individualism, and the latter will accompany it as its legitimate negation up to their blessed end.

Past History

"Did Thucydides," asks the classicist Simon Hornblower, "ever envision a time when civilized human beings would not speak what we call ancient Greek?" Because he clearly did not, anthropologists have always been prepared to back Herodotus as "the father of history." Herodotus recounted all the tales, tall and short, that the "barbarians" told him: an ethnographic bent that appealed to anthropologists, but led the less credulous historians to consider him rather "the father of lies." Add into the comparison Thucydides' belief in a self-interested human nature and the rational-realism of IR politics, and you will see why he has been the model of Western historiography ever since. So if Anthropology was for too long the study of "history-less peoples," history for even longer was studying "cultureless peoples."

Fortunately, all that past history is also past Anthropology, if not vice versa.

Borrrrrrring!

Thomas Kuhn and others have wondered whether the social sciences have paradigms and paradigm shifts like the natural sciences. Nothing seems to get concluded because some say that the natural sciences don't even have them, and others that in the social sciences you couldn't tell a paradigm from a fad. Still, considering the successive eras of functional explanation of cultural forms—first, by their supposed effects in promoting social solidarity, then, by their economic utility, and lately, as modes of hegemonic power—there does seem to be something like a Kuhnian movement in the social sciences. Though there is at least one important contrast to the natural sciences.

In the social sciences, the pressure to shift from one theoretical regime to another, say from economic benefits to power effects, does not appear to follow from the piling up of anomalies in the waning paradigm, as it does in natural science. In the social sciences, paradigms are not outmoded because they explain less and less, but rather because they explain more and more—until, all too soon, they are explaining just about everything. There is an inflation effect in social science paradigms, which quickly cheapens them. The way that "power" explains everything from Vietnamese second person plural pronouns to Brazilian workers' architectural bricolage, African Christianity or Japanese sumo wrestling. But then, if the paradigm begins to seem less and less attractive, it is not really for the standard logical or methodological reasons. It is not because in thus explaining everything, power explains nothing, or because differences are being attributed to similarities, or because contents are dissolved in their (presumed) effects. It's because everything turns out to be the same: power. Paradigms change in the social sciences because, their persuasiveness really being more political than empirical, they become commonplace universals. People get tired of them. They get bored.

In fact power is already worn out. Borrrring! As the millennium turns over, the new eternal paradigm *du jour* is identity politics. The handwriting is on the wall: I read where fly-fishing for trout is a way the English bourgeoisie of the late nineteenth century developed a national identity. "In nineteenth century England, fishing, not less than war, was politics by other means," writes anthropologist Richard Washabaugh in a book called *Deep Trout*. (Is this title a play on Clifford Geertz, so to speak, or on "Deep Throat"?) Well, the idea gets at least some credibility from the fact that fishing is indeed the most boring sport on television. Coming soon: the identity politics of bowling, X-games, women's pocket billiards, and Nascar racing.

Double Identity

Those who talk a lot about identity politics often practice it in the way they talk about it. (You know what I mean.)

Know Thyself

Anthropologists generally live in the most capitalistic and commodified societies in the world. Along with all other human scientists, including cult studs, they tell us that capitalism and commodification are hegemonic forces cum discourses that enslave people to particular ontologies or regimes of truth: notably those that resolve persons and the objects of their existence to exchange values. But do anthropologists, living under the worst of such regimes, really experience themselves as culturally unfree? And how could they even conceive, let alone experience, cultural differences, the otherness of others? Hegemony is supposed to determine not only what one thinks but also what one cannot think. This makes Anthropology a performatic contradiction of the latest cultural theory.

There is a certain species of academic whiffle bird that is known to fly in ever-decreasing hermeneutic circles until it flies up its own backside.

The Political Economy of the Humanities

Anthropologists have become the working-class of the Cultural Studies movement. Relegated to the status of ethnographic proles in the academic division of labor, they are the ones condemned to long days, months and years of dirty and uncomfortable (field) work. Their minds numbed by laboring on obdurate cultural realities, they leave higher theory to English professors. These cult studs are the thinking class, an emancipated (and emancipating) literati, while anthropologists are content to be the subaltern clients of their hegemonic discourses.

Anthropologists of the world unite...

An Empire of a Certain Kind

Rallying the Athenians after a second year of war with the Spartans, the second year of the Peloponnesian War, Pericles warned his countrymen that they were not only in peril of losing their empire but of suffering "from the animosities incurred in its exercise." "For what you hold," he told them, "is, to speak somewhat plainly, a tyranny. Perhaps it was wrong to take it, but it would be dangerous to let it go." Tyranny abroad was the work of the first and (some would say) the greatest democracy known to history. But then, the same sort of contradiction between freedom and subjugation inhabited Athens' domestic politics, where immigrants, slaves and their descendants, as well as women, were denied many of the democratic privileges enjoyed by the minority of the population, the full male citizens.

The Athenians developed an empire of a distinctive kind—and distinctively disposed to brew up a volatile mixture of attraction and humiliation among the people dominated by it. It was not like the European colonial empires of modern times that physically imposed their own state on other territories and societies. Gained by invasion and maintained by occupation, such imperial states were actually sovereign over the subject peoples, governing them with all the necessary means of administration, regulation and compulsion. But the Athenian empire was domination without administration. In many ways it was an empire of signs—signs of power: magnificent, draconian or both at once, that brought other states more or less voluntarily into submission, perhaps for their own advantage and protection but surely on pain of their destruction. Athens did not directly rule the others, but everywhere she could she intervened in local politics, often by force or by show of force, to create proxy democracies that would be like and compliant with her own. Imperialism as a democratic mission. Many of the tributary cities were nominally "allies," culturally bound to Athens by common heritage (as Ionian Greeks) and politically bound in a League of which she was the hegemon. Securing the sea routes and the resources of trade, the empire was the political condition of the great commercial enterprise that made Athens the richest and most populous city-state of the Hellenic world. In turn the wealth the Athenians drew from the empire went into the displays of high culture and brute force by which they kept it under control.

The marvelous and the murderous: an empire of domination without administration works largely by demonstration-effects of its power. On the one hand, Athens was a spectacle of culture that functioned—to adopt a Hobbesian phrase of governance—"to keep them all in awe." Such was the politics of this glory that was Greece: the magnificence of her architecture and art, the brilliance of her theater, the glittering processions and ceremonies, the Academy and the Agora, the gymnasia and the symposia. "Our city," boasted Isocrates, "is a festival for those who come to visit her." Subject cities notably visited her with their annual tributes at the time of the principal religious festival, the City Dionysia, which was also the theater season. Even those who never saw Athens could know her superiority by the reputation of her writers and philosophers, her politicians and her athletes. Almost inevitably, then, her greatest enemy, oligarchic Sparta, opposed her by a strategy of cultural negation: adopting a material fundamentalism and a puritanical moralism that denied the values Athens knew as civilization. A mere collection of old-fashioned villages, Sparta, commented Thucydides, could show no measure of her fame in the poverty of the remains she would leave for posterity; whereas, the ruins of Athens in time to come would make her power seem twice as great as it actually was. On the other hand, those who were not awed by Athens' glory, who did not acknowledge her superiority or revolted against it, would feel her sting—again by way of demonstration.

In the empire of signs, force too is a sign of force, perhaps the most effective if not always the most economical, aiming to induce the fear and obedience of the many out of the brutal example made of the few. So argued the bellicose Cleon, urging the Athenians to respond to the revolt of the allied city of Mytilene by exterminating the lot of them. "Punish them as they deserve," he said, "and teach your allies by a striking example that the penalty of rebellion is death." In this case, a counter argument (to the same exemplary effect) that it would be unwise to kill the innocent common people, who were everywhere Athens' natural democratic allies, limited the Athenians to the slaughter of the 1000 or so Mytilinean aristocrats they held responsible. But in the famous case of Melos, a Spartan colony that would not submit to the Athenians, offering instead to remain neutral and friendly to them, the outcome was much less fortunate. Your friendship, the Athenians told them, would only be "an argument to our subjects of our weakness." This was the sixteenth year of the Peloponnesian war, well after the Mytilene affair, when demonstrations of Athenian might and resolve were taking on more and more strategic value. So now, delivering an ultimatum to the Melians, they in effect said, you're either with us or you're against us. If states maintain their independence, it means they are strong, and if "we do not molest them it is because we are afraid; so that beside extending our empire, we should gain in security by your subjection." Counting on the justice of their cause and the feckless hope that the Spartans or the gods would save them, the Melians refused to surrender, and were wiped out. All the men were killed, all the women and children sold into slavery. Not that they hadn't been warned of Athens' will to power. "Of the gods we believe," the Athenians told them, "and of men we know, that by a necessary law of their nature they rule wherever they can."

Thus driven by a desire of power after power, the Athenians in the end overreached themselves, and they lost everything. They had gotten to the point where it seemed they would collapse if they could not expand. "We cannot fix the exact limit at which our empire shall stop; we have reached a position in which we must not be content with retaining what we have but must scheme to extend it, for if we cease to rule others, we shall be in danger of being ruled ourselves." So spoke Alcibiades in winning the approval of the Athenian assembly for the grandiose Sicilian campaign that ended in complete disaster, and set the course of empire toward decline and defeat. But already at the beginning, nearly fifty years before the Peloponnesian war, when the Athenians, in beating off the Persian menace, discovered their own destiny as a sea power, they set in motion a geopolitics of expansion that was almost a formula for spinning out of control. Increasing rule of the seas meant developing the commercial power that would deliver the necessary money, materiel and manpower; as conversely, increasing commerce meant developing the maritime-military strength necessary to secure it. Democratic Athens became a predatory power. Yet its burgeoning population and business soon made it dependent on critical energy imports from barbarian (i.e., non-Greek) lands situated at the limits of its military force: the rich food grains of distant Sicily, Egypt, and the Crimea. Placed at the center of a sphere of domination that was thus moving outward in many directions, Athenian interests, costs and dangers were all subject to geographic multiplication on the order of the square of the radius of an expanding circumference times 3.14159. To meet its difficulties, Athens could put pressure on fellow Greeks, as by turning allies into tributaries, or she could find new barbarians to conquer. In either case, the empire that brought well being in the homeland spread humiliation and resentment abroad. Caught in a vicious cycle of expansion and repression, Athens could be generally detested in the same degree she became glorious and admired.

The Peloponnesian war was a testimony to this cycle of domination and resistance—and over time, exaggerated it. As opposed to the incidents that set it off, the war's "truest cause," as Thucydides said in a famous passage, "was the growing power of the Athenians and the fear this inspired in the Spartans." If the war then required the Athenians to further exploit their "growing power," it also offered their subjects new possibilities of revolt and (Spartan) liberation. Cleon's warning to the Athenians in the fifth year of the conflict was even stronger than Pericles'—"your empire is a despotism and your subjects disaffected conspirators"—and events did not prove him wrong. At the end of the war, as the Spartans under Lysander closed in on their besieged and starving city, the Athenians, as Xenephon said, mourned for their loss and still more for their fate, as they feared they would be dealt with as they had dealt with so many other peoples. All Greece rejoiced to see this city fall and those they had driven out of their own cities now restored to them. Thucydides tells us that he did not set out to write a history merely in order to please the immediate public. He dared to hope his recounting of the Peloponnesian war would "last forever"—inasmuch as human histories of this kind were sure to happen again. So he would be content, he said, "if these words of mine are judged useful by those who want to understand clearly the events which happened in the past and which, in the course of human things, will at some time or other and in much the same ways, be repeated in the future." (*Social Analysis*, Spring 2002)

World-Historical Best Selling Book Title

Publishers used to speculate a lot about what would be the best selling book title in the business. For a long time the best by consensus was "Lincoln's Doctor's Dog." I was trying to think what would do for the human sciences these days. My candidate would be "The Neoliberal Ontology of the Anthropocene."

Re the Selfish Gene and other Forms of Bourgeois Self-regard

The simple and universal fact of the incest taboo signifies that the incorporation of otherness is an essential condition of human identity and being.

Ethnology as Western Ontology

The myriad ethnographic statements of the form, "The So-and-So believe that...," typically referring to something Europeans would disbelieve, should actually be written, "The So-and-So know that..." To cite Jean Pouillon, "It's the non-believers who believe that the believers believe."

What is anthropology but Talmudic exegesis by non-believers?

Chances of Success

There are two categories of people who generally have no realistic idea of their chances of success: politicians and authors.

The Gift of Everyone to Everyone

When native Australians or New Guineans say that their totemic animals and plants are indeed their kinsmen, that these species are persons like themselves, and that in offering them to others they are giving away part of their own substance, we have to take them seriously, which is to say empirically, if we want to understand the large consequences of these facts for how they organize their lives. The graveyard of ethnographic studies is strewn with the remains of reports that, due to the anthropologists' own presuppositions of empirical fact, were content to ignore or debunk the Amazonian peoples who said that the animals they hunted were their brothers-in-law, the Africans who told that they systematically killed their kings when they became weak, or the Fijian chiefs who claimed they were gods. So we have to follow the reasoning of those Australian Aboriginals for whom eating their own totem animals or plants would be something like incest or self-cannibalizing, even as they ritually nourish and protect these species for other people's use. We thus discover a society the opposite in principle of the bellicose state of nature that Hobbes posited as the primordial condition—an idea of the inherent human condition, moreover, which is still too much with us. Instead of a "war of every man against every man," each opposing the others in his own self-interest, here is a society organized on the premise of everyone giving himself to everyone.

Still, *on aura toujours des problemes.*

Natural Science and Human Science

The human scientist is not in a relation of a thinking person to a mute object of interest; rather, anthropologists and their like are of the same intellectual nature as the peoples they study—our alters and our interlocutors. Indeed, inasmuch as these peoples are meaningfully making their modes of life, and inasmuch we share the same capacities of symbolic invention and understanding, we have the possibility of knowing the cultures of others in ways that are in some respects more powerful than the ways natural scientists know physical objects. As Claude Levi-Strauss once put it: "Of all the sciences, anthropology is without a doubt unique in making the most intimate subjectivity into a means of objective demonstration."

Consider that by contrast, the more the natural scientist discovers about things, say the table on which I am working, the less such things are like anything in human thought or experience. Despite appearances to the contrary, science shows there are spaces within and between the molecules that compose it; and beyond that, at the level of quantum mechanics, our knowledge of things defies all common sense of space and time. For an elementary quantum example, we have to accept that the same object is in two different places at the same time. More systematically, descriptions of quantum realities consist of complex equations that include arcane symbols not on my computer keyboard. Niels Bohr is often quoted as saying that, "if you are not shocked by quantum physics, you don't understand it."

I don't really understand it. Still, I do know that many

peoples consider that brothers and sisters are composed of the same ancestral being. How did they do that? Actually, given their symbolic capacities, it's easy for people to be in two different places at the same time. All you have to do is daydream. You could even share substance with or be related to yams, supposing, say, that they were growing in the same place as your ancestors were buried.

If natural science starts out with what is familiar to our experience and ends with something altogether remote, human science works the other way around. One may well begin with something so distant or even so unpleasant to us as cannibalism in the Fiji Islands (during the 19th century), yet end up by finding it "logical"—which is, after all, a mental state of our own. In 1929, the British anthropologist A.M. Hocart recounted the formal speech of a Fijian chief presenting a reward to the carpenter who had built his fine canoe. The chief apologized that he could not offer the carpenter a "cooked man" or a "raw woman," for Christianity, he explained, "has spoiled our feasts." The "cooked man" refers to an enemy cannibal victim, the "raw woman" would be a virgin daughter of the chief offered as a wife. One immediate anthropological question this poses is why the woman should be equivalent to the cannibal victim? The brief answer is that they have the same finality or function, which is the beneficial reproduction of the society: the woman directly by bearing children, the cannibal victim as a sacrifice whose consumption in concert with the god procures divine benefits, notably in agricultural and human fertility. But then, the great canoe for which these are appropriate payments is itself a sacred (taboo) vessel, carrying a temple on board as it is sailed in quest of foreign bodies in war or prized valuables in trade. Further, given the relationship of raw women to cooked men, one can understand why in some parts of Fiji a fine war club is a necessary betrothal gift, in effect compensating the family for the future loss of their daughter by the anticipated gain of an enemy victim. Enough said? This cannibalism is becoming logical, and logic is something going on inside ourselves. Pardoning the pun, a custom that began as strange and remote as cannibalism in the South Seas has been assimilated and internalized —that is, as our own good sense.

Since cultural practices are meaningfully constructed, and since we ourselves are symbolizing beings, we have the privilege of knowing others by reproducing in the operations of our own mind the very ways they are culturally organized. The method and the content of investigation are one: the most intimate subjectivity becomes the means of an objective demonstration. Of course, this is not the only way of knowing others. By the same token of our symbolic capacities we can also treat them as physical objects; and surely, as in archaeology, we necessarily know them by their physical works. But we won't get the same knowledge of the symbolically ordered ways of human life, of what culture is, or even the same empirical certainty.

On a Friend's Hospitalization in Australia

Hospitals are like cold baths: you should get in and out of them as quickly as possible. I don't know about Oz, but hospitals in the US are the third worst cause of mortality, after cancer and heart disease. The whole idea of a hospital is crazy: putting all those sick people together and then creating a circulating vector of disease among them in the form of the nursing staff. That's why they call it "staff infection."

Is the Notion of Ideology Ideological?

Commenting on the death of the Roman Emperor Commodus, the great Edward Gibbon wrote:

> Such was the fate of the son of Marcus, and so easy was it to destroy a hated tyrant who, by the artificial powers of government, had oppressed, during thirteen years, so many millions of subjects, each of whom was equal to their master in strength and personal abilities.

So is kingship any more real, less ideal, or even more lethal than religion?

Perhaps it was when the Romans became relativist and historical about the existence of their own and other peoples' gods that the divine became a matter of belief rather than knowledge, and we were set on our way to the present human science of the gods as discursive epiphenomena of politics. The gods were reduced to the status of man-made ideas, by contrast to and dependent on a coercive sovereign power—as if the former were not an essential condition of the latter. The so-called superstructure is not an idealized afterthought or functional commentary on sovereignty, but in nature and practice an *a priori* constituent of power. It is a fundamental aspect of an entirely human-made, cultural apparatus that, in allowing one man no superior in endowments than others to nevertheless govern their fate, Gibbon accordingly called "the artificial powers of government."

The gods are no secondary formation on kingship—they are found even in chiefless societies—and sovereignty is no less a cultural construction than divinity. There are no human social powers that are not symbolically constituted. So is the average common academic notion of ideology itself ideological? It may well be that in significant respects, the false consciousness is in our human sciences.

Human Political Power is the Usurpation of Divine Power

I am speaking here of the myriad peoples who know "spirits" (so-called) as true and act on that knowledge, and not, as in current functionalist dispensations, reduced to an epiphenomenal discourse that imitates, mystifies, or otherwise upholds the human powers-that-be. This is simply ethnographic realism, not some philosophical idealism. In these societies, the gods, ancestors, species masters, and other metapersons *are* the powers-that-be, often without equivalents in the structures of the human order. They are the means and models for, rather than reflexes of, human authorities: even kings are in origin imitations of gods rather than gods of kings.

We need something like a Copernican revolution in the sciences of society and culture: a shift in perspective from human society as the center of a universe onto which it projects its own forms–that is to say, from the received Durkheimian, Marxist, and structural-functionalist conventions—to the ethnographic realities of people's dependence on the encompassing metaperson-others who rule earthly order, welfare, and existence. The human community is a subordinate part of a cosmic polity.

For Durkheim, god was an expression of the power of society: people felt they were constrained by some greater authority, but they knew not whence it came. But if what has been said here has any cogency, it is better said that god is an expression of the lack of power of society.

Finitude is the universal human predicament: people do not control the essential conditions of their existence. If people really controlled their own lives, they would not die. Or fall sick. Nor do they govern the weather and other external forces on which their welfare depends.

The life-force that makes plants and animals grow or women bear children is not their doing. And if they reify it—as *mana*, *semengat*, *hasina*, or the like—and attribute it to external authorities otherwise like themselves, this is not altogether a false consciousness, though it may be an unhappy one. Vitality and mortality do come from elsewhere, from forces beyond human society, even as they evidently take some interest in our existence....

But so far as the relation between the cosmic authorities and the human social order goes, in both morphology and potency there is no equivalence between them. As we have tried to show especially by egalitarian and chiefless societies, many of them remote from states and their religions, neither in structure nor practice do they match the powers above and around them. Among these societies there are no human authorities the likes of Sedna and Sila of the Central Inuit, Ungud of western Australian Aborigines, the Original Snake of Malay Peninsula people, Afek and Magalim of Telefomin, Nankui of the Amazonian Achuar, or the Sky People of the New Guinea Highlands. What Viveiros de Castro says in this regard to the Arawete and Tupi Guarani peoples generally can be widely duplicated among the classically "acephalous" peoples:

How to account for the coexistence of, on one hand, a "loosely structured" organization (few social categories, absence of global segmentation, weak institutionalization of interpersonal relations, lack of differentiation between public and domestic spheres) with, on the other hand, an extensive taxonomy of the spirit world...an active presence of that world in daily life, and a thoroughly vertical "gothic" orientation of thought...Societies such as the Araweté reveal how utterly trivial any attempts are to establish functional consistencies or forced correspondences between morphology and cosmology or between institution and representation...

We should not be quick to write off the human dependence on gods, ancestors, ghosts or even seal-persons as so much mistaken fantasy. Of course, nobody nowadays is going to attribute these notions to a "primitive mentality." And from all that has been said here, it cannot be claimed these beliefs in "spirits" amount to an ideological chimera perpetrated by the ruling class in the interest of maintaining their power—that is, on the Voltairean principle of, "There is no God, but don't tell the servants." Here we do have gods, but no ruling class. And what we also distinctively find in these societies is the coexistence in the same social reality of humans with a variety of metahumans who have life-giving and death-dealing powers over them. The implications look to be world-historical. As is true of big-men or shamans, access to the metaperson authorities on behalf of others is the fundamental political value in all human societies so organized. Access on one's own behalf is usually sorcery, but to bestow the life-powers of the god on others is to be a god among men. Human political power is the usurpation of divine power.

Counterfeit Coin

As I see it, the US counterinsurgency (COIN) strategy—as practiced in Iraq and Afghanistan—consists of
two main tactics, combat and bribery. But since these
tactics are aimed at populations that are culturally and
socially opaque to those who must implement them, it
has seemed necessary to bring in a new sort of intelli-
gence agent, namely academics versed in such matters,
to provide a more rational employment of firepower
and treasure. That I believe is the primary purpose of
the notorious Human Terrain project. By mapping the
composition and relationships of the local population,
including their political dispositions and economic
desires, the embedded anthropologists, sociologists,
and their ilk will be able to target military firepower
more effectively and/or identify the people who can be
bought off. Essentially these academics would operate
according to the practices outlined in the recent US
Counterinsurgency Manual, the principles of which are
largely credited to General Petraeus. Incidentally what
was not credited in the *Manual* were whole chunks of
text that were plagiarized from sociological and anthropological sources, mostly of mediocre quality. Also
notable was the publication of a trade edition of the
Manual by the University of Chicago Press, which
although it failed to vet the text (thus allowing the
plagiarism to pass), was content to make a profit without honor in its own country.

The potential good news, at least for the targeted
populations, is that the prescriptions of Petraeus' counterinsurgency doctrines, as set forth in the *Manual*, are
absurd, let alone completely unworkable. What the

Manual prescribes is that the military staffs, and in some measure personnel at all echelons, must understand the people. To understand the people, they need analytic knowledge of six "sociocultural factors": society, social structure [you can already see the incoherence], culture, language, power and authority, and institutions. To understand the social structure, they will have to know the existing groups, institutions [again], organizations and networks. "Groups" are defined as two or more people who interact on the basis of shared expectations of behavior and have interrelated statuses and roles. To identify relevant groups inside and outside the area of operations, the commanders of combat units should be supplied with information on formal relations between groups, informal relations between groups, divisions and cleavages within groups, and cross-cutting ties between groups. That's just "groups," there's also institutions, organizations, and networks.

Then, after similar "mapping" of institutions, organizations and networks, the military staffs "should identity and analyze the cultures of the society as a whole and each major group within the society." This minor research proposal includes inquiry into how the world is categorized as well as prevailing values, beliefs (core, intermediate and peripheral), attitudes, perceptions, identities, norms, codes of behavior, rituals, symbols, ceremonies, myths, narratives, taboos, and something called "cultural forms," which are "concrete expressions of belief systems." Further, having mastered the social structure and the culture—I'm not sure what happened to the "society" rubric—there remains the small matter of the system of power: "staffs must determine how power is apportioned and used within a society."

No need to go into the other imaginary research agendas, such as learning the local languages and the people's "interests." The fact is it would take dozens of anthropologists with many years of training and even more years of fieldwork to do all this, by which time pretty much everything would be different, especially at the tactically relevant level of appearances. (Among the other things the military intelligentsia doesn't understand about anthropology is that it is the only discipline apart from high-energy physics that is committed to the study of disappearing objects.) Moreover, being operational, much of this cultural knowledge has to be acquired by ordinary combat troops who generally have no more than secondary school education: exactly how much knowledge they will need and what kinds the *Manual* does not specify, but presumably enough to engage and manipulate the people for better or for worse. Given the already demonstrated ineptitude of Human Terrain specialists, who as a rule have no in-country experience, the soldiers' instructors are also likely to be mediocre. The new counterinsurgency doctrine turns out to be a hopelessly disorganized course in introductory anthropology offered by inept professors to the academically challenged students in a combat zone who will presumably ace the multiple-choice final exam by guessing at the right answers and shooting the alternatives.

Unfit to Print

A selection from a collection of rejected letters to the editor of *The New York Times*.

To the Editor:

Regarding Gail Collins' "The Joys of Political Sex," if only those who are without sin were allowed to cast the first vote, there would be no congressional legislation at all. (12/10/09)

To the Editor:

Regarding "Marines Invest in Local Afghan Projects..." (Jan 30), it has been evident for some time that, for all the anthropological talk of learning the local culture in order to win hearts and minds, the principal counterinsurgency weapon of the US in Iraq as well as Afghanistan has been money. The Marine captain arrives at a forward counterinsurgency base with a briefcase containing $25,000 in Afghan currency to pay off local "contractors." We call this tactic "development," although it would be more honestly described as "bribery," and in view of its usual distribution in favor of local elites it is also more recognizable as "corruption."

Anyhow it's cheaper than paying off American contractors, the likes of Haliburton, KBR or Blackwater. So never mind the words, let's just quickly "buy" enough time to get out of there. (1/30/10)

To the Editor:

Regarding the story of March 27 on the recent Iraq elections, your reporters observe that claims of fraud on the part of parties that see their fortunes change in the slow vote count make "an ominous reminder of an Iraqi political culture where winning is everything and compromise elusive." And what about American culture in this regard? What about the refusal of the losing Republican party to compromise or even participate in democratic government, and the incitements to violence that followed Obama's victory, now doubled and tripled with the passage of health care reform?

One might say that we are all Iraqis now, except that it is evident that the US policy of promoting elections in ethnically, religiously, and economically divided states is a certain method of deepening the existing divisions and pushing the society toward a state of nature. Here indeed winning is everything, so the situation in countries where we would impose our politics—and indeed our culture—is even worse than ours. Adding global causes-to-die-for, such as "democracy," "freedom," and "good versus evil" to local disputes makes them all the more unconditional and insoluble. The same goes, of course, for Afghanistan. When will we learn? (3/17/10)

To the Editor:

The *Times* (Oct. 24) reports the Iranians are giving bundles of cash to Karzai aides. Also as described in the same issue, American private security forces in Iraq pay off civilians to keep them from reporting random acts of killing. Performing military duties that range from KP to combat, and killings that include Iraqi and US forces, these private armies, aka mercenaries, outnumber the American combat troops in the Middle Eastern War zones. Meanwhile American construction companies reap huge profits from so-called development projects that in Iraq have largely failed to provide adequate electricity—although a sufficient amount to electrocute American soldiers taking showers.

In both Iraq and Afghanistan, payoffs from these development projects have made rich men of numerous tribal and government leaders. Members of Karzai's government are also profiting handsomely from the drug trade in Afghanistan. The American project of buying off tribal leaders, known in Iraq as "The Awakening," has turned into a major counterinsurgency strategy. COIN was a well-chosen acronym for the military's counterinsurgency policy, insofar as it largely consisted of bribery. The policy is now failing in Iraq, however, because the Shiite-dominant government refuses to continue buying off Sunni Awakening members, even as payments from insurgent groups take up the slack.

War may be politics by other means, but it is now economics by the same means. (11/23/10)

To the Editor:

Mrs. Clinton's lecture to Middle Eastern governments (Jan. 14) in effect advising them to be more like us is rather contradictory to the prevailing sense of American exceptionalism. After all we are unique, there can be none like us. How can others hope to imitate our gender and racial equality, our democracy free of corruption by wealth or corporate power, our immunity to political assassinations, our concern for the health and welfare of the poor, and the other things that make us uniquely happy and good? (1/14/11)

To the Editor:

You gotta laugh (almost) at the hypocrisy. According to the report "Business Payoffs Helped Gaddafis Solidify Control" (March 24), American-based companies doing business in Libya acceded to Col. Gaddafi's demand for payments so that he could make blood-money compensation for the downing of Pan Am Flight 103. This, according to American officials, reflected "a Libyan culture rife with corruption, kickbacks," and the like. And what about the American businesses concerned? Or most recently, the conduct of our big financial institutions even after their recent scandalous dealings in mortgages and derivatives? (3/24/11)

To the Editor:

Report has it that the decision of Egypt's Muslim Brotherhood to run a presidential candidate "is likely to unnerve the West and has already outraged Egyptian liberals" (*NYT*, April 1 2012). Taken together with conditions in Libya and Syria, it seems that the Arab Spring is like the one in Chicago, where as the saying goes, "if Spring comes, Winter can't be far behind."(4/1/12)

To the Editor:

As corporations, airline companies are persons. Airline companies may legally merge. Therefore, same sex marriage is legal. (7/12/12)

To the Editor:

On the eve of the tenth anniversary of the American invasion of Iraq, we are told ("10 Years Later, an Anniversary Many Iraqis Would Prefer to Regret") the U.S. has succeeded in turning the country into a factionally divided society with a malfunctioning government that has lost any sense of national identity. What goes around comes around. Instead of recreating Iraq in the image of American democracy, it seems we have recreated America in the image of the divisive Iraqi state. To a large extent as a consequence of the Iraq war, our own Sunni Republicans are now engaged with our Shiite Democrats in an unconditional factional struggle that is paralyzing our national government and undermining our national identity. (3/19/13)

To the Editor:

In "U.S. Colleges Finding Ideals Tested Abroad" (December 12), Stanford Dean, Richard Saller, and several other U.S. college administrators justify their Chinese ventures with the tired old saw of spreading liberal values in an anti-democratic regime. Aside from merely disguising their large overseas investments in money and academic vainglory, their pious claims of working from the inside are content to ignore that they have embedded their own schools in institutions under the surveillance and control of a Chinese Party-State with a known history of severe restrictions on academic freedom. One is reminded of the story of the two black-hooded medieval executioners leaning on their long axes and talking of their work, in which one says to the other, "The way I see it, if I didn't do this, some SOB would get the job."

By their partnerships with Chinese universities and their branches in Chinese cities, American schools become accomplices of an anti-democratic power far more than they are able to speak truth to it. Indeed the truth is that U.S. institutions of higher learning are becoming more and more like multinational corporations, complementing a similar monetization of the academy at home with a competition in international branding. (12/12/13)

To the Editor:

In the 2008 presidential campaign, Sarah Palin was haunted by "The Bridge to Nowhere." In the 2016 campaign, Chris Christie will be haunted by "Nowhere to the Bridge." (12/17/13)

To the Editor:

The studies that reportedly "show a little bit of Neanderthal in us all" may underestimate the significance of that supposedly little bit. Especially the studies suggesting "that Neanderthal genes involved in skin and hair were favored by natural selection in humans. Today they are very common in living non-Africans." Would this imply that the so-called "primitive" Neanderthals were the white people, in contrast to the more "advanced" *Homo sapiens* from Africa? From the point of view of contemporary racism, the paleontological implication would be something more than skin deep. (1/10/14)

To the Editor:

Surely the G.O.P. politicians of anti-abortion convictions who are arguing about the meaning of "natural born citizen" in the US Constitution are debating the wrong issue. They should be concerned about where a prospective candidate for the presidency was conceived rather than where he or she was born, since by their lights life begins at conception. What if the candidate were conceived in Mexico, Canada, Russia, or the Fiji Islands? On the other hand, what the debate does unequivocally confirm is that according to the Founding Fathers, as stipulated in the Constitution, human life begins at birth, not at conception. (2/3/16)

To The Editor:

It appears that Mr. Trump is suffering from a compounded form of Attention Deficit Disorder: he not only cannot focus, but he cannot get enough attention. (7/21/16)

To the Editor:

The U.S. Presidency, L.L.C. is the best business investment the Trump family cartel ever made. And again
they did it primarily with other people's money—
campaign contributions. (5/9/17)

To the Editor:

The presidency of Donald Trump is making it all too
clear that the hallowed doctrine of "a government of
laws and not men" is an insufficient basis for the preser-
vation of a democratic republic. Missing from that
doctrine is a necessary third term: the traditional
conventions of a democratic society. As Harvard political scientist Steven Levitsky tells us, the breakdown of
democratic regimes around the world is "much more
about the underlying informal norms than about the
formal rules." In just this way, the dramatic firing of
the FBI Director James Comey is the latest in a cascad-
ing series of moves by Mr. Trump that, while not ille-
gal, effectively undermine the principles of democratic
government. From threatening to jail his opponent
during the election, to using the presidency to enhance
his personal fortune and distributing key positions of
government to his own family members, Mr. Trump's
regime is more reminiscent of a classic third world
dictatorship than the classic American republic.

We are being made rudely aware that democracy does
not consist simply in a constitution and representative
government. Already during the Trump transition,
more than one Washington insider was surprised to
learn how much our political system was based on

custom rather than law. But there is a long scholarly tradition, from Alexis de Tocqueville's *Democracy in America* to the work of Professor Levitsky and colleagues, demonstrating that a democratic government is founded on a democratic society of customs, rules, norms, and ethics—or else, it fails. Democracy is a culture. (5/14/17)

Culture is the Human Nature

My first anthropology mentor, Leslie White, used to say, "No ape can appreciate the difference between holy water and distilled water"—because there is no difference, chemically, although the meaningful difference of "holy" makes all the difference about how people value and use it, and whether or not they are thirsty makes no difference in this regard. It was a succinct lesson in what means "symbol" and what is "culture." In relation to the so-called human nature, leading a life according to culture means having the ability and knowing the necessity of realizing our bodily dispositions and requirements symbolically: that is, according to the meaningful determinations of ourselves and the objects of our existence in the specific schemes of a given society.

These biological dispositions in the human species, however, are indeterminate unless and until they are meaningfully and variously ordered in different cultural schemes. In a way, the Amazonians and other peoples who take culture as the original human state and the body as secondary and conditional are quite correct. The paleontological record would support them, inasmuch as culture is much older than *Homo sapiens*, many times older, and culture was a fundamental selective condition of the species' development. The evidence for culture among hominids goes back two or three million years; whereas, anatomically modern *Homo sapiens* is only about 50,000 or 100,000 years old. For millions of years, humans have been fashioned in and for a cultural existence. They have had to culturalize their animality. Not that humans are or ever were

so-called "blank slates," lacking any biological impera-
tives. Only that what was uniquely selected for in the
genus *Homo* was the encompassment of these impera-
tives in various forms of meaning, hence the ability to
satisfy, sublimate, repress or otherwise organize them
in the myriad ways that archaeology, history and
ethnography have documented.

Notice that I am not denying the currently popular
doctrine of "co-evolution": the happily uncontroversial
answer-that-lies-somewhere-in-between biology and
culture, inasmuch as biological and cultural develop-
ments have mutually conditioned each other. But it
does not follow that the effect of the co-evolution was
an equal valence of these "factors" in human social
existence. On the contrary, there had to be an inverse
relation between the variety and complexity of cultural
patterns and the specificity of biological impulses. In
the co-evolution, the development of culture, and
more particularly the development of cultural differences, would have to be complemented by the depro-
gramming of what used to be called instinctual behav-
iors. The consequence was the organization of biological functions in diverse social forms. Biological dispositions became such according to the ways they were
symbolically constituted and culturally practiced. We
have the equipment to live a thousand different lives, as
Clifford Geertz observed, although we end up living
only one. This is only possible on the condition that
biological needs and drives do not specify the particular
way they must be expressed.

Take sexuality, for example. What is most revelatory
about the relation between culture and biology is not
that all cultures have sex but that all sex has culture.

Sexual desires are variously expressed and repressed according to local cultural determinations of appropriate partners, times, places, and bodily practices. We subordinate our generic sexuality in all kinds of ways—including transcending it in favor of higher values of celibacy, which also proves that in symbolic regimes there are more compelling ways of achieving immortality than the mindless mystique of the so-called "selfish gene." (After all, immortality is a symbolic phenomenon—what else could it be?) Or again, consider that some Western people even have sex by telephone. Or for yet another example of conceptual manipulation (pun intended), there is Bill Clinton's famous, "I did not have sexual relations with that woman."

As it is for sex, so for other inherent "needs" or "drives": nutritional, aggressive, sociable, compassionate—whatever they may be or however conceived, they came under symbolic definition and cultural order. Aggression or domination may then take the behavioral form of, say, the New Yorker's response to "Have a nice day"—DON'T TELL ME WHAT TO DO. We can war on the playing fields of Eton, give battle with swear words or insults, dominate others by giving them gifts that cannot be reciprocated or writing scathing reviews of their books.

When the moral philosophers of the Scottish Enlightenment, Adam Ferguson especially, took up the cause of human will against predetermined sin or instinct, they added a social dimension that set the course to an anthropological understanding of human nature as a culturally informed becoming. Ferguson went beyond the usual defense of free will: the argument that moral agency would be meaningless if we cannot not sin. (It's like Isaac Singer said: "You have to believe in free will. You have no choice.") For Ferguson, man was truly a social animal, formed in society rather than opposed and pre-posed to it. In society we are born, he said, and there we remain, capable of all the sentiments, good or bad, by which peoples constitute their ways of life:

> If we are asked therefore, where is the state of nature to be found? We may answer: It is here; and it matters not whether we are understood to speak in the island of Great Britain, at the Cape of Good Hope, or in the Straits of Magellan.

I conclude: the state of nature, it is here—and there: everywhere and every how that people are. Culture is the human nature.

The Original Political Society

Even the so-called egalitarian and loosely structured societies known to anthropology, including hunters such as Inuit or Australian Aborigines, are in structure and practice subordinate segments of inclusive cosmic polities, ordered and governed by divinities, ancestors, species masters, and other such metapersons endowed with life and death powers over the human population. "The Mbowamb spends his whole life completely under the spell and in the company of spirits" (Vicedom and Tischner). "[Arawete] society is not complete on earth: the living are part of the global social structure founded on the alliance between heaven and earth" (Viveiros de Castro). We need something like a Copernican revolution in anthropological perspective: from human society as the center of a universe onto which it projects its own forms—that is to say, from the Durkheimian or structural-functional deceived wisdom—to the ethnographic realities of people's dependence on the encompassing life-giving and death-dealing powers, themselves of human attributes, which rule earthly order, welfare, and existence. For Hobbes notwithstanding, something like the political state is the condition of humanity in the state of nature; there are kingly beings in heaven even where there are no chiefs on earth.

On the So-Called Economic Basis

In a brilliant passage on "production" in *Beyond Nature and Culture*, Philippe Descola observes that the notion of an heroic individual working creatively on inert matter, thereby transforming it into a useful existence by his own effort according to his own plan, does not describe an intersubjective praxis in which metaperson alters are the primary agents of the process.

How long will it take the human sciences to conceptually absorb the fact that indeed there is no such thing as "production" in the majority of societies known to anthropology and history, those generally known as "premodern"? People are not responsible for the output of their work, certainly not in the primary subsistence sectors: they do not create their material means of existence, but receive them from the "spiritual" sources who generate, control, and bestow them. One could say that "the spirits own the means of production," were it not that the so-called "spirits" are essentially human in character and intentions—they are so many metapersons—and as the animate beings of plants, animals, and places, they ARE the means of production. Accordingly, as has been pointed out by Descola, Tim Ingold, Eduardo Viveiros de Castro, and many others, so-called "production" is an intersubjective negotiation with the metaperson powers-that-be: from which it also follows that the political credit of material success goes to those—elders, shamans, chiefs, garden magicians, kings—who have privileged access to the "spirits," and not necessarily or at all to those who do the work. The alienation of the workers was not invented by capitalism.

Stranger-King Formations

(From the Introduction to *On Kings*, David Graeber and Marshall Sahlins, Hau Books, 2017)

Stranger-kingdoms are the dominant form of pre-modern state the world around. The kings that rule them are foreign by ancestry and identity. The dynasty typically originates with a heroic prince from a greater outside realm: near or distant, legendary or contemporary, celestial or terrestrial. Alternatively, native rulers assume the identity and sovereignty of exalted kings from elsewhere and thus become foreigners—as in the Indic kingdoms of Southeast Asia—rather than foreigners becoming native rulers. The polity is in any case dual: divided between rulers who are foreign by nature—perpetually so, as a necessary condition of their authority—and the underlying autochthonous people, who are the "owners" of the country. The dual constitution is constantly reproduced in narrative and ritual, even as it is continuously enacted in the differential functions, talents, and powers of the ruling aristocracy and the native people.

The kingdom is neither an endogenous formation nor does it develop in isolation: it is a function of the relationships of a hierarchically ordered, inter-societal historical field. The superiority of the ruling aristocracy was not engendered by the process of state formation so much as the state was engendered by the *a priori* superiority of an aristocracy from elsewhere—endowed by nature with a certain *libido dominandi*. The ruling class precedes and makes a subject class.

On his way to the kingdom, the dynastic founder is notorious for exploits of incest, fratricide, patricide, or other crimes against kinship and common morality; he may also be famous for defeating dangerous natural or human foes. The hero manifests a nature above, beyond, and greater than the people he is destined to rule—hence his power to do so. However inhibited or sublimated in the established kingdom, the monstrous and violent nature of the king remains an essential condition of his sovereignty. Indeed, as a sign of the metahuman sources of royal power, force can function politically as a positive means of attraction as well as a physical means of domination.

For all the transgressive violence of the founder, however, his kingdom is often peacefully established. Conquest is overrated as the source of "state formation." Given their own circumstances—including the internal and external conflicts of the historical field—the indigenous people often have their own reasons for demanding a "king to lead us and to go out before us and fight our battles" (1 Samuel 8:20). Even in the case of major kingdoms, such as Benin or the Mexica, the initiative may indeed come from the indigenous people, who solicit a prince from a powerful outside realm. Some of what passes for "conquest" in tradition or the scholarly literature consists of usurpation of the previous regime rather than violence against the native population.

While there is frequently no tradition of conquest, there is invariably a tradition of contract: notably in the form of a marriage between the stranger-prince and a marked woman of the indigenous people—most often, a daughter of the native leader. Sovereignty is embodied and transmitted in the native woman, who constitutes the bond between the foreign intruders and the local people. The offspring of the original union—often celebrated as the traditional founder-hero of the dynasty—thereby combines and encompasses in his own person the essential native and foreign components of the kingdom. Father of the country in one respect, as witness also his polygynous and sexual accomplishments, the king is in another the child-chief of the indigenous people, who comprise his maternal ancestry.

Even where there is conquest, by virtue of the original contract it is reciprocal: the mutual encompassment of the autochthonous people by the stranger-king and of the king by the autochthonous people. The installation rites of the king typically recreate the domestication of the unruly stranger: he dies, is reborn, and nurtured and brought to maturity at the hands of native leaders. His wild or violent nature is not so much eliminated as it is sublimated and in principle used for the general benefit: internally as the sanction of justice and order, and externally in the defense of the realm against natural and human enemies. But even as the king is domesticated, the people are civilized. The kingship is a civilizing mission. The advent of the stranger-king is often said to raise the native people from a rudimentary state by bringing them such as agriculture, cattle, tools and weapons, metals—even fire and cooking, thus a transformation from nature to culture (in the Lévi-Straussian sense). As has been said of African societies, it is not civilized to be without a king.

As allegorized in the original union, the synthesis of the foreign and autochthonous powers—male and female, celestial and terrestrial, violent and peaceful, mobile and rooted, stranger and native, etc.—establishes a cosmic system of social viability. In a common configuration, the autochthonous people's access to the spiritual sources of the earth's fertility is potentiated by king's conveyance of fecundating forces, such as the rain and sun that make the earth bear. Each incomplete in themselves, the native people and foreign rulers together make a viable totality—which is what helps the kingdom to endure, whatever the tensions of their ethnic cum class differences.

Although they have surrendered the rule to the foreign king, the native people retain a certain residual sovereignty. By virtue of their unique relation to the powers of the earth, the descendants of the erstwhile native rulers are the chief priests of the new regime. Their control of the succession of the king, including the royal installation rituals, is the warrant of the foreign-derived ruler's legitimacy. In the same vein, the native leaders characteristically have temporal powers as councilors of the stranger-king, sometimes providing his so-called prime minister. To a significant extent, the principle that the sovereignty of the king is delegated by the people, to whom it belongs by origin and by right, is embedded in stranger-king formations, hence widely known before and apart from its early-modern European expressions.

Notwithstanding the superiority and perpetual foreign ethnicity of the ruling aristocracy, they are often not dominant linguistically or culturally, but are assimilated in these respects by the indigenous population. Correlatively, the identity of the kingdom is usually that of the native people.

European colonization is often in significant aspects a late historical form of indigenous stranger-kingship traditions: Captain Cook, Rajah Brooke, and Hernando Cortes, for example.

The Political Economics of Pre-modern Kingdoms

(From the Introduction to *On Kings*, David Graeber and Marshall Sahlins, Hau Books, 2017)

Kingship proprietary schemes are complex. On one hand the country is divided into local properties, of which the ancestors of the inhabitants, or the indigenous spirits with whom the ancestors have made a pact, are the "true owners"—and the decisive agents of the area's fertility. Correlatively, the local subject population, who have ritual access to these metaperson authorities through their initiated elders or priestly leaders are themselves deemed the "owners," the "earth," the "land," or some such designation of their founder rights to the country relative to the ruling aristocracy—especially in the ubiquitous stranger-kingdoms where the latter are foreign by origin and ethnic identity. Although possessory in relation the rulers, the local people's rights are only usufructory in relation to the spiritual inhabitants, whose ultimate ownership must be duly acknowledged by the current occupants. (Notice that these relations between the local people and the autochthonous spirits are themselves analogous to the larger structure of the stranger-kingdom.) On the other hand, the ruling aristocracy and the king—who by tradition may have been poor and landless originally except as they were granted land by the native people—may also be "owners"; but here in the sense of lordship over large landed estates and their inhabitants, giving them tributary rights to a portion of product and manpower generated by the underlying population. Whereas the subject people's relation to the process is productive, by virtue of their control of the primary means, the rulers' relation to the process is extractive, by virtue of their domination of the producing people. As the East African Nyoro people put it: "The Mukama [the king] rules the people; the clans rule the land" (from John Beattie).

Accordingly, the kingdom economy has a dual structure, marked by fundamental differences between the *oikos* economics of the underlying population and the specifically political economics of the palace and aristocracy, undertaken with an eye toward the material subsidization of their power. Devoted rather to a customary livelihood, the primary sector is organized by the kinship and community relations of the subject people. The ruling class is principally concerned with the finished product of the people's work in goods and manpower, on which it takes a toll that helps fund an elite sphere of wealth accumulation, oriented particularly to the political finalities of strengthening and extending its sphere of domination. Labor in this sphere is organized by corvée, slave, and/or client relations. Beside support of an imposing palace establishment, it is notably employed in the accumulation of riches from extramural sources by means of raid, trade, and/or tribute. Employed then in conspicuous consumption, monumental construction, and strategic redistribution—and possibly on further military exploits—this wealth has subjugating effects, both directly as benefiting some and indirectly as impressing others. Moreover, the material success of the king is the sign of his access to the divine sources of earthly prosperity, thereby doubling the political effects of his wealth by the demonstration of his godly powers.

Kingship is a political economy of social subjugation rather than material coercion. Kingly power does not work on proprietary control of the subject people's means of existence so much as on the beneficial or awe-inspiring effects of royal largesse, display, and prosperity. The objective of the political economy is the increase in the number and loyalty of subjects—as distinct from capitalist enterprise, which aims at the increase of capital wealth. To paraphrase a Marxian formula, the essential project of kingship economics is P-W-P'—where the political command of people gives an accumulation of wealth that yields a greater command of people—by contrast to the classic capitalist formula, W-P-W'—where the proprietary control of productive wealth (capital) gives the control of people (labor) in the aim of increasing productive wealth.

Structure and Event

Structure on one hand, agency and contingency on the other, are not opposed historical determinants in the sense that they exclude one another. On the contrary, each is the condition of the historical possibility of the other. In authorizing particular persons and circumstances as historical difference-makers, the structural order is a *sine qua non* of their efficacy, though it is not responsible for their particularities, nor then for the difference they will make. In Sartrian terms, particularity is an irreducible way of living universality or the structure of the collectivity; and accordingly the collectivity must live through the attributes of the persons and things on which it has made itself dependent. Hence the possibility of historical outcomes that are structurally consistent and evenementially variable. Between the structural order of the historical situation and what actually happens there is no necessary relation. Rather, the structure is realized in a particular historical form by the mediation of the contingencies it has empowered. So while one may justly conclude that the transcendent potencies ascribed to James Brooke allowed him to become the Rajah of Sarawak, *he could have just as easily been assassinated for the same reason*—by a rival Malay leader, for example, or some Dayak headhunter. (Perhaps nowhere more than in Dayakland, uneasy lies the head that wears the kingly crown.) Brooke's death would have followed from, and realized, the same concepts of the potency of alterity that had made him the rajah—for they also defined his enemies. Indeed, in an analogous instance of the exaltation of the stranger, Captain Cook was killed by Hawaiians after he was venerated as a manifestation of an ancient deity. Note that in either event, the divinization of the powerful stranger or his assassination, would be structurally consistent. One might say that the structure is a sufficient but not a necessary condition of the outcome.

Atemporal Dimensions of History

"Life, after all, is as much an imitation of art as the reverse." So commented Victor Turner in regard to the way Central African Ndembu villagers applied principles from the traditions of Lunda kingship they had learned as children to their current social relations. Or again, how important political leaders likewise inform and structure their own public actions by the relations encoded in dynastic epics. The past is not simply prologue, but as Turner says, it is "paradigm." Historical causes in the mode of traditions have no temporal or physical proximity to their effects: they are inserted into the situation, but they are not of it. Embedding the present in terms of a remembered past, this kind of culturally instituted temporality is a fundamental mode of history-making from the omnipresent Dreamtime of Australian Aboriginals to the state politics of African kings. But then, what actually happens in a given situation is always constituted by cultural significations that transcend the parameters of the happening itself: Bobby Thomson didn't simply hit the ball over the left field fence, he won the pennant. The better part of history is atemporal and cultural: not "what actually happened," but what it is that happened.

Where Have All the Cultures Gone?

What happened to Anthropology as the encompassing human science, the comparative study of the human condition? Why is a century of the first hand ethnography of cultural diversity now ignored in the training and work of anthropologists? Why are graduate students in the discipline ignorant of African segmentary lineages, New Guinea Highlands pig feasts, Naga head-hunting, the kula trade, matrilateral cross cousin marriage, Southeast Asian galactic polities, Fijian cannibalism, Plains Indian warfare, Amazonian animism, Inuit kinship relations, Polynesian mana, Ndembu social dramas, the installation of Shilluk kings or Swazi kings, Azande witchcraft, Kwakiutl potlatches, Australian Aboriginal section systems, Aztec human sacrifice, Siberian shamanism, Ojibwa ontology, the League of the Iroquois, the caste system of India, Inner Asian nomadism, the *hau* of the Maori gift, the religion of the Ifugao, etc. etc. We are the custodians of this knowledge, and we are content to let it be forgotten. Where else in the university are these things to be taught, or is it that they are not worthy of scholarly contemplation, and should just be confined to the dustbin of intellectual history?

Maybe in a few hundred years, if the human species survives the dark ages of planetary degradation, there will be a cultural renaissance driven by the discovery of some buried or flooded libraries filled with astonishing memoirs of human achievement.

David Brooks

To the G-S tune of "I am the Very Model of a Modern Major General":

I am the very model of a public intellectual.
My op-eds in the New York Times are never ineffectual.
I'm expert in all matters from political to sexual,
I am the very model of a public intellectual.

Emeritus Rants

Academia is the pursuit of disinterested knowledge by self-interested individuals.

Lévi-Strauss looms larger with each passing anthropological degeneration.

Good anthropology is thirty years out of date.

Academic immortality is way overrated. By the time you achieve it, you're already dead.

Two things are certain in the long run: that we'll all be dead and we'll all be wrong. Obviously, a good career is when the first comes before the second.

Still, longevity is a good career move. It's better than the alternative.

On age: 85 is not the new 60. It's the new 84. For that reason, conversations among emeritus professors should have a five-minute limit on organ recital.

Clifford Geertz observed to me about aging academics: First your teachers die. Then the baseball players die. Then your colleagues die. And finally…no one cites you.

Still, retirement has its compensations, as I heard Fibber McGee say: You can work in the morning, and you have all afternoon to look for your glasses.

What's wrong with Facebook? Coupled to the uninteresting verbal selfies, everything serious—political or intellectual—has a half-life of 12 hours. It's an internet cyclotron for disappearing mental objects. Postmodernity lives.

Kiss of Death

David Brooks hypes Bourdieu in the *NYT*. Probably it's not the first time Brooks Bourdieu.

On Existence

I think, therefore I am, said Descartes.
I also think.
Therefore, I am Descartes.

Haiku

On any Sunday morning we live in interesting *New York Times*.

Culture in Colonial and Academic Practice

In relation to colonialism, the concept of "culture", as deployed both practically and academically, has had a checkered career. Certainly from the 1980s (and still?), anthropologists, for whom culture had once been the central object of their science, largely condemned it in no-uncertain, moral-political terms. Culture was "the essential tool for making others," a means of "incarcerating others in their difference," a concept for "producing the other...and racism has always been an integral part of it;" indeed:

> the anthropological concept of culture might never have been invented without a colonial theater that both necessitated the knowledge of culture (for the purposes of control and domination) and provided a colonized constituency that was particularly amenable to "culture."

Culture thus being in bad repute, a number of alternative terms were adopted to do its still-necessary work: "discourse," "subjectivity," and even the curious suggestion that we should keep "cultural" as an adjective and drop "culture" in the nominative.

On the other hand, if colonialism was responsible for the anthropological concept of culture, it was also from the beginning to now conceived as an anti-colonial concept. From its origins in the Germanic counter-enlightenment to its current militant adoption by the colonized and erstwhile-colonized peoples, "culture" was opposed to imperialism as the essence of self-determination and freedom. "The [German] princes speak French," lamented Johann Gottfried v. Herder, "and soon everyone will follow their example; and then, perfect bliss, the golden age when the world will speak one tongue…There will be one flock and one shepherd. National cultures, where are you?" Indeed in time the German people suffering the incursion of French *civilsation* and indigenous peoples around suffering Western imperialism responded in similar ways, by taking consciousness of their own, distinctive culture—by way of defending it. Then again, Herder laid the ground of the anthropological uses of *Kultur* by also defending the indigenous cultures: "ye men of all nations of the globe, who have perished in the course of ages; ye have not lived and enriched the soil with your bodies so that at the end of time your posterity should be made happy by European civilization." Only a real misanthrope, he said, would take European culture as a universal standard. Yet Herder not only understood the similarity between the plight of the colonized peoples and that of his own society, he envisioned the anthropology that would ultimately evolve from this imperial history: "Our technologies are multiplying and improving; our Europeans find nothing better to do than run all over the world in a kind of philosophical frenzy. They collect material from the four corners of the earth and will someday find what they were least looking for: clues to the history of the most important part of man's world."

Two centuries later, the peoples from the four corners of the earth who deployed their "culture," "kastom," "cultura," or some equivalent defense against their domination and exploitation were making good on the prophecy. For Amilcar Cabral, founder of the African Party for the Liberation of Guinea and Cape Verde, martyr that cause, the anti-colonial struggle was a culture war. Inasmuch colonialism itself is a massive system of cultural hegemony, he wrote, culture "has proved to be the very foundation of the liberation movement." By reclaiming control of their own existence, the people thereby recuperate their own historicity. Because a society "that really succeeds in throwing off the foreign yoke reverts to the upward paths of its own culture, the struggle for liberation is above all an act of culture." Regrettably that has not yet happened in Guinea-Bissau.

I leave it to Norbert Elias and others to examine the historicity that motivated the German intellegensia to develop the culture concept, and Matti Bunzl and other intellectual historians to trace the path of the culture concept through the nineteenth century and into its realization in American anthropology through Franz Boas. As I say, its colonial and anti-colonial reverberations have been complex in these regards: including the paradox that the anthropologists most intimately involved in colonial government, the British social anthropologists and their counterparts elsewhere in the Commonwealth, had the least developed notion of what culture is, confining merely it to ideal, historically arbitrary means of maintaining the social structure, the real object of their study.

Apres Moi, Le Deleuze

As I said, don't be Saussure. I wouldn't Lacan to that theory. I thought it Bourdieu to death. There's too much Deleuze. Better, have you ever seen Latour de France? I met him in a Balibar, of all places. Enough Said. ■

Also available from Prickly Paradigm Press:

continued

continued